INCLUSIVE HOUSING
A Pattern Book

Design for Diversity and Equality

W. W. Norton & Company

New York • London

in association with

The Center for Inclusive Design & Environmental Access

School of Architecture & Planning

University at Buffalo, The State University of New York

The illustrations, tables, data, and other information herein are original works, have been obtained, or were reproduced based on many sources. The Center for Inclusive Design and Environmental Access has made every reasonable effort to make this reference work accurate and authoritative, but also not warrant, and assume no liability for, the accuracy and completeness of the illustrations, text, drawings, tables, data, or other information, nor their fitness for any particular purpose. It is the responsibility of the users to apply their professional knowledge in the use of information contained in this book, to consult the original sources for additional information when appropriate, and if they are not a professional architect, to consult with a professional architect or engineer when appropriate. Further, the drawings presented herein are for illustrative purposes only and are not to be used for construction purposes. The Center for Inclusive Design and Environmental Access does not warrant that the suggestions and examples illustrated herein are compliant with any applicable codes, laws, or other governing document in any particular jurisdiction. It is the responsibility of the user to ensure the suggestions of this book meet all applicable codes in their project's respective jurisdictions prior to adapting them for construction.

The Center for Inclusive Design and Environmental Access does not endorse any particular product, service, builder, architectural firm, or any other commercial entity mentioned or depicted herein.

Inclusive Housing A Pattern Book Design for Diversity and Equality
Authors: Edward Steinfeld and Jonathan White With contributions from: Danise Levine, Jordana Maisel, Heamchand Subryan, John Sepples, Danielle McCrossen, Stephanie Koch, David Schoell

Copyright © 2010 by Edward Steinfeld and Jonathan White

For information about permission to reproduce selections from this book, write to Permissions, W. W. Norton & Company, Inc., 500 Fifth Avenue, New York, NY 10110

For information about special discounts for bulk purchases, please contact W. W. Norton Special Sales at specialsales@wwnorton.com or 800-233-4830

Manufacturing by Courier Kendallville
Book design by the IDEA Center
Electronic production: Joe Lops
Production manager: Leeann Graham

Library of Congress Cataloging-in-Publication Data

Steinfeld, Edward.
 Inclusive housing : a pattern book : design for diversity and equality
/ authors, Edward Steinfeld and Jonathan White ; with contributions
from Danise Levine ... [et al.]. — 1st ed.
    p. cm.
 Includes bibliographical references and index.
 ISBN 978-0-393-73316-7 (pbk.)
 1. Architecture—Human factors. 2. Architectural design.
3. People with disabilities—Housing. 4. Sustainable urban
development. I. White, Jonathan (Jonathan Robert), 1985–
II. Levine, Danise R. III. Title. IV. Title: Design for diversity
and equality.
 NA2542.4.S74 2010
 728'.0103—dc22

                                2010000256

ISBN: 978-0-393-73316-7 (pbk.)

W. W. Norton & Company, Inc., 500 Fifth Avenue,
New York, N.Y. 10110
www.wwnorton.com

W. W. Norton & Company Ltd., Castle House,
75/76 Wells Street, London W1T 3QT

0 9 8 7 6 5 4 3 2 1

Foreword

Truly sustainable neighborhoods that have remained stable over time are those that have a diverse range of housing types and a diverse population. This includes people across a wide range of incomes, with different lifestyles and family situations, and different ages and degrees of mobility. In many of the most beloved of such traditional neighborhoods, it is possible for people to start out as young singles in cool apartments over clubs and shops, move a few blocks to a large apartment appropriate for a couple, move around the corner to a small house, then around another corner to a larger one, and then when physical mobility is limited, move back to a cool apartment over clubs and shops.

We are now living longer than in any time in history. As the average age of our population increases, we need to create and support neighborhoods that provide a diverse housing stock that enables people to age in place. Although this concept can mean aging in the same house, it is even more important to provide ways in which people can find an appropriate dwelling type for different stages of life in the same neighborhood.

In her last book, *Dark Age Ahead,* Jane Jacobs described the impact of a socially supportive neighborhood on the aging. During the devastating heat wave of a few years ago, there was a significantly higher death rate in neighborhoods in which elders were isolated in single buildings than in those in which they interacted with other people and had access to local institutions and services, especially retail. A lifelong association with neighbors provides social capital that is part of the support system of people dependent on others because of frailty or functional limitations.

This book makes several important contributions to ways in which the design of dwellings can support the creation of such lifelong, sustaining neighborhoods:

First, it defines an important aspect of inclusive housing that is often overlooked in the literature on this subject. While other marginalized populations need design attention, housing and neighborhood designs that address diversity in ability benefit everyone, so it is a truly inclusive goal. Disablement is an experience that all groups share. In fact, disability is more prevalent among minorities, low-income individuals, and homeless people than among the rest of the population.

Second, the book highlights the value of an inclusive design approach with respect to the great demographic shift toward an older society. The concept of designing housing for the lifespan is one that no developer, architect, or builder can ignore any longer. The market for housing is changing radically due to this shift, and this book provides the tools to address it.

Third, the book explores accessible design in the context of urbanism, traditional neighborhood and housing design, privacy, security, and sustainability. It provides useful tools and patterns for achieving good urbanism and good design while providing access for all. These techniques and concepts were debated in many forums over the past several years, including several sessions of the Congress for the New Urbanism. The neighborhood is considered by practitioners of traditional housing design to be the essential building block of towns and cities. The qualities of a good neighborhood include the provision of a diverse range of dwelling types and many of the services needed for daily life within a compact and walkable environment. This calls for innovative design that combines higher density with human scale, complicating the effort to provide a substantial stock of accessible dwellings. Through debate and collaboration, the authors and many practitioners of traditional urbanism and housing found new solutions, many of which are represented in this book.

Most importantly, this book demonstrates that issues of accessibility and visitability are not limited to the dwelling unit. An accessible house in an automobile-dependent community does not provide accessibility for those who are not able to drive—an increasingly significant population as we age. The creation of compact, human-scale neighborhoods with easy access to a diverse range of services provides the framework for people to establish a truly sustaining neighborhood—one in which people look after one another. The design of the neighborhood, the street, the block, and the individual lot are critical in providing the context within which the goals of inclusive housing can be realized. If accessibility is considered while designing the neighborhood, the needs of a diverse population are much easier to address at the scale of the dwelling.

—Raymond Gindroz
co-founder and principal, Urban Design Associates
Board of Directors, Congress for the New Urbanism

Contents

SECTION 1 | INTRODUCTION

This section describes the purpose and scope of this book and describes how to effectively use and apply its information.

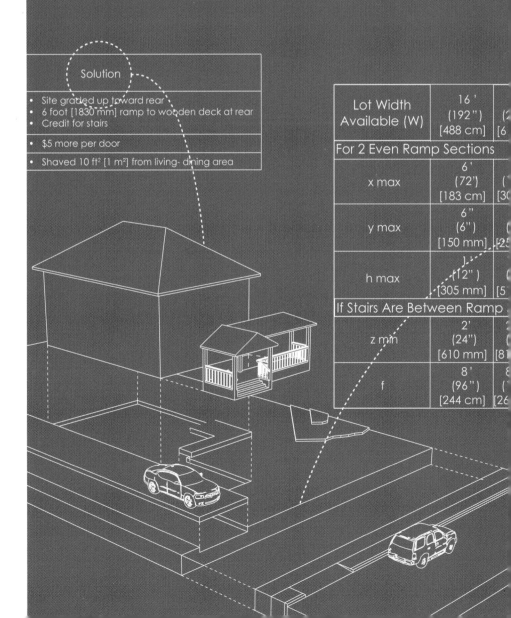

Solution
• Site graded up toward rear
• 6 foot [1830 mm] ramp to wooden deck at rear
• Credit for stairs
• $5 more per door
• Shaved 10 ft² [1 m²] from living- dining area

Lot Width Available (W)	16 ' (192") [488 cm]	
For 2 Even Ramp Sections		
x max	6 ' (72') [183 cm]	
y max	6 " (6") [150 mm]	
h max	1' (12") [305 mm]	
If Stairs Are Between Ramp		
z min	2' (24") [610 mm]	
f	8 ' (96") [244 cm]	

Purpose

This book is a resource for designing communities that accommodate social diversity and provide equitable opportunities for all residents. It focuses on design of housing that provides accessibility to people with disabilities and, at the same time, benefits all other residents. The book emerged out of a lengthy discussion with proponents of traditional neighborhood development (TND) about accessible housing design in the urban context. This discussion identified the need for information that would help incorporate accessibility for people with disabilities into neighborhood and housing design practices without compromising other important design goals. TND advocates promote neighborhood-based development as an alternative to sprawl through the adoption of historically proven approaches to community planning, urban design, and housing design. They share many goals and ideas with other advocates who support smart growth, livable communities, and design for aging in place. These groups propose that we should design communities that are not only environmentally sustainable but also socially sustainable, communities in which any individual can expect to access a full range of civic resources and engage fully in social and domestic life. Planners, developers, architects, engineers, public officials, investors, and community activists are all involved in these movements. Organizations with interests in socially sustainable communities include the Smart Growth Network and the Congress for the New Urbanism (CNU), advocacy groups for older people like the AARP (formerly the American Association of Retired People), the Urban Land Institute, and the Green Building Council. The CNU Charter (www.cnu.org/charter) gives a particularly compelling vision of the socially sustainable city of the future.

Form-based zoning rather than single-use zoning supports the incorporation of mixed-use buildings like these in Abacoa, FL

These principles for diversity and accessibility are found in the Charter:

▶ Neighborhoods that are diverse in use and population;

▶ Communities that are designed for the pedestrian and public transit as well as the car;

▶ Cities and towns that are shaped by physically defined and universally accessible public spaces and community institutions;

▶ Urban places that are framed by architecture and landscape design that celebrate local history, climate, ecology, and building practice.

As these principles illustrate, advocates of TND, smart growth, and livable communities usually emphasize universal access for public spaces and community institutions, but neglect access to housing. They are not alone in neglecting this issue. Most new housing in the U.S. is inaccessible to people with disabilities. Yet, people with mobility, sensory, and cognitive impairments form a significant portion of the population. There have been many estimates of the proportion of the population with a disability. In a recent global study, after comparing many sources of data, researchers concluded that about 15% of the population has a disabling condition (World Health Organization, 2006). In addition, we must consider that people with disabilities live in social groups, so their families and friends experience disablement through everyday social life. For example, if a family wants to invite a relative with a disability to a party or just for dinner, they need to have an accessible home. Another recent study examined the likelihood that each house would be the residence of a person with a mobility impairment (Smith, Rayer, and Smith, 2008). The authors concluded that, over the course of a dwelling's useful life, there is a 25% chance that any individual house will have a resident with a disability. The rapid growth of the older segment of the population will increase the attention that disability must receive in the community of the future since it will increase the prevalence of disability.

This book is one small effort toward affecting a change in design practices. It provides concrete strategies for designing inclusive communities – specifically, places that are accessible to people with a broad range of physical and cognitive abilities, including older residents. The heart of the inclusive design idea is that design can transform our perception that difference is only about "them" to an understanding that design for diversity benefits all of us. In the process of changing perceptions, something unexpected happens. We will find that what is good for one group of people usually has benefits for the rest of us. While this book focuses on difference related to physical, sensory, and cognitive ability, the lessons can certainly be applied to other issues of diversity like race, income, and gender. Thus, the focus of this book does not minimize the importance of social barriers on creating barriers to full participation in community life. We hope it will encourage others to develop resources like this to address those issues.

While emphasizing urban patterns of neighborhood development, the book is certainly useful for application to all kinds of housing

Example of a traditional neighborhood at Beacon Hill in Boston, MA

Example of a traditional, low-income, high-density community at Oak Hill in Pittsburgh, PA

New Urbanist community in Baldwin Park, FL

in all types of neighborhoods. In fact, it addresses trends that have widespread significance in the residential construction market. Throughout the world, efforts are underway to find better ways to build new and revitalize old communities. The goals are to develop livable and healthy neighborhoods, reduce urban sprawl, reduce reliance on fossil fuels, and ensure that the benefits of thoughtful urban design are equitably distributed. This book will demonstrate that accessible housing design is quite compatible with these goals, and, in fact, is necessary to achieve them.

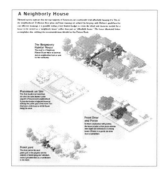
Habitat for Humanity Pattern Book

This book utilizes tools that planners and urban designers have developed for neighborhood planning and housing design. One such tool is the pattern book. Pattern books are guidebooks for use in controlling the design of housing to ensure that houses constructed in a locality fit with a desired character and contribute to the convenience, safety, and sociability of neighborhoods. A second tool, the SmartCode, is a form-based planning tool that is adopted by communities, in conjunction or as a replacement for conventional zoning and planning guidelines, to implement traditional neighborhood development. It is also adopted on a voluntary basis by land developers.

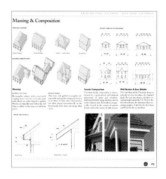
Gulf Coast Pattern Book

This pattern book is different than most. Pattern books usually focus on one region, community, or neighborhood. Good examples are the pattern books created to help in the rebuilding of Gulf Coast communities (see mississippirenewal.com and louisianaspeaks.org). But pattern books can also be developed for a building type or a target market. For example, a recent project completed by Urban Design Associates and the Institute for Classical Architecture for Habitat for Humanity, "A Pattern Book for Neighborly Houses," was developed to help Habitat chapters around the country improve the design of small affordable homes in inner-city neighborhoods by adopting a contextual approach to design (http://www.classicist. org/resources/habitat-pattern-book). This book is similar in that it focuses on a single design issue but presents guidelines and ideas that can apply to a wide range of contexts.

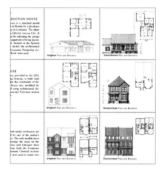
Louisiana Speaks Pattern Book

In this book, we use the Transect, an element of the SmartCode, as a means to explore the relationship between house, lot, block, and neighborhood. The Transect is a concept that classifies neighborhoods by their mix of land uses, density, and general character. Certain types of housing are appropriate for each classification.

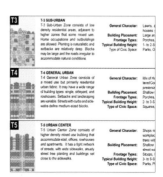
SmartCode & Manual

This book, like the SmartCode, recognizes that, to achieve the goals of urbanism, it is necessary to consider the total picture. The house must fit on the lot; the lot must fit in the block; the block must fit with the character of the neighborhood. We have included examples that cover a wide range of housing types, styles, and development densities. Thus, we adopted a "context-sensitive" approach to accessible design. Rather than present some stock solutions that ignore the context of real projects and other design goals, this book explores how accessibility can be implemented in different types of neighborhoods and housing forms, all with the goal of achieving high-quality urban places.

The Transect illustrates six categories, or prototypical zones, of land use based on density ranging from natural environments to urban cores. This book focuses on housing in three of these zones: T3 – Suburban, T4 – General Urban, and T5 – Urban Center. The T6 – Urban Core zone was not included because almost all housing in this zone would be elevator equipped and as such presents no unique problems in accessible design. The T1 – Natural zone and T2 – Rural zones were not included for a similar reason – the low density development in these zones presents no additional challenges than one would find in the T3 zone because lot sizes are so large that providing accessibility on the site is relatively easy through adjustments in finished grades during construction. The character of the T3, T4, and T5 zones would be typical of a medium to large city and its immediate suburbs.

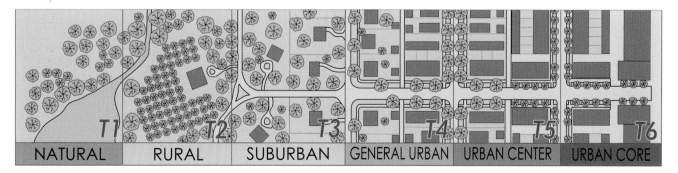

Plan view transect diagram based on SmartCode & Manual p. SC81

The three Transect Zones we have included can be described as follows:

▶ T3 Suburban represents the context of a first ring suburb, but it is also characteristic of single-family neighborhoods within city limits. Detached houses on streets designed to balance convenient use of vehicles with pedestrian needs are typical in this zone. Vehicular access to lots could occur from the street or alleys. Off-street parking is provided on each lot for more than one car. Services, access to public transportation, and recreation facilities would be located within walking distance. Apartments in this zone are accessory units such as carriage houses or are located in small buildings that look similar to large houses. Lot sizes are relatively large with ample setbacks and most lots have driveways. There are sidewalks at the sides of all streets. Some streets may be cul-de-sacs off feeder streets.

T3 Suburban Transect Zone

▶ T4 General Urban represents residential neighborhoods with a higher density. Here, a mixture of housing types are found. Streets accommodate vehicles but they are designed to favor pedestrians. Vehicle access to individual lots is usually limited to curbside or to the rear of the lots. More commercial and civic facilities are available in this zone than in the T3 zone. The houses include a range from large single-family detached types on larger lots, to higher density single-family buildings like attached houses or townhouses and small apartment buildings. Setbacks are minimal. Civic and commercial land uses are provided on major streets. There may be some mixed-use buildings like live-work units. Parkways or boulevards integrate recreational spaces into streetscapes. There may be squares and mews interspersed in the urban fabric.

T4 General Urban Transect Zone

▶ T5 Urban Center features mixed-use buildings on pedestrian-friendly commercial streets. Parking is provided on the street or on the site in lots or in garages. There may be neighborhood garages that serve houses within walking distance. Density is higher than in the T4 zone and there are more commercial and civic land uses. There are no single-family detached dwellings or small apartment buildings. High-density low-rise buildings are the most common building form. Setbacks are minimal or nonexistent. Commercial land uses are more extensive and mixed-use buildings are common in commercial areas. All streets have sidewalks, but park strips and boulevards are less common. Urban squares and piazzas may be provided.

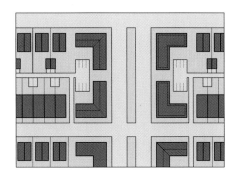

T5 Urban Center Transect Zone

In addition to exploring the implications of accessible design for different urban zones, we also examined a range of building types that are commonly found in each of the zones:

▶ Single-family houses are emphasized because they are not currently covered by federal accessibility codes so there is very little guidance on how to introduce accessibility to this building type.

▶ Small apartment buildings with 4–8 units are included because reports from the field suggest that some architects and developers argue that the Fair Housing Act Accessibility Guidelines (FHAAG) restrict the use of some building types of this size that are valuable in traditional neighborhood development. Thus, we wanted to illustrate how easy it is to apply the FHAAG without restricting building design.

▶ We included some less common building types that present some interpretation issues in the application of regulations. These include small mixed-use buildings with apartments above commercial spaces, live-work units, and courtyard buildings.

Scope

The first sections of this book address general concepts of accessibility, neighborliness, and their relationship to good urban housing and neighborhood design. The next set of sections provides illustrated guidelines for different approaches to block, lot, and house designs. The book concludes with examples of complete house designs illustrated on typical lots. In each section, the goals of accessible design and related design issues are identified, and good practice solutions are illustrated. Technical guidelines and selected construction details are included that are sympathetic with a traditional approach to housing and site design. We have also developed and included some useful design tools. A section on "How to Use This Book" is included to explain the book's structure further. All the single-family examples included in the book include Visitability provisions and many have additional accessibility features. Multifamily examples (more than 3 units) are designed to comply with the Fair Housing Accessibility Guidelines. Each of the example building designs has a style that is common in at least one region of the country. We included enough diversity so that we could illustrate how accessibility can be achieved in different ways without compromising aesthetics, livability, or neighborliness.

How to Use This Book

The book treats the block, lot, and house as sets of components of a total "assembly" that generates a neighborhood character. There are many options for each set of components but they work together in certain specific ways. For example, the decision to have alleys in a block eliminates the need for driveways, allows houses to be closer together, and reduces the backyard depth. This means that design for privacy and territoriality are more important than in other contexts and thus makes some house forms more appropriate for the lots than others. The result is a neighborhood character that is distinctly different from a block with no alleys where each house has its own driveway. Each assembly presents different challenges for accessibility and each challenge must be addressed appropriately to produce a neighborly house that fits with its context.

The book is conceived so that it can be used most effectively as a design companion. Readers should become familiar with the entire book. Then, during design, use the book as a reference and guide throughout the design process.

Step 1: Identify Your Design Constraints & Goals

Before attempting to use the tools this book provides, designers and planners should have a clear understanding of the goals and constraints of a particular project. Are you designing for a high-density or low-density neighborhood? Is the lot size and proportion a given, or is it flexible? What building types will be included? What is the topography of the site and to what degree can it be altered?

Goals:
2 bedroom, 1 bath
Fully accessible 1st-floor
1st-floor bedroom
On-site parking
Alley access?
On-grade access

Constraints:
30 ft. lot width
$110,000 budget
900-1200 max. ft²
10 ft. min. setback
Flat site

	New Construction	Solution
No-step Entry	No cost	• Site graded up toward rear • 6 foot [1830 mm] ramp to wooden deck at rear • Credit for stairs
Widen Interior Doors	$25	• $5 more per door
Bathroom Expanded	No cost	• Shaved 10 sf [1m²] from living- dining area

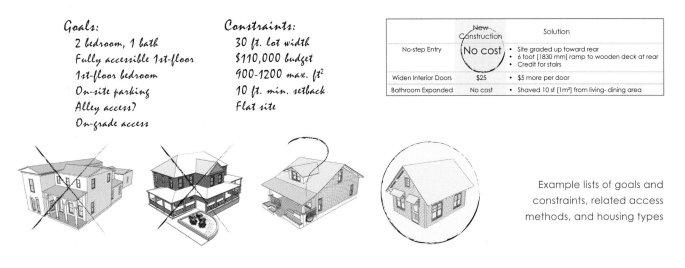

Example lists of goals and constraints, related access methods, and housing types

Step 2: Study the Components

Study and identify what block, lot, and house components you want to use. Features such as grading, driveways, walkways, ramps, stairs, and porches all work together to create a synergistic whole. For example, steep sloping streetscapes may require certain combinations of building position, vehicle access, or even plantings to create an accessible community with an appropriate character for its context. Knowing your design goals from Step 1 will help determine which optional features to consider and which ones to dismiss.

Block Components

Block components such as the block layout, topography, type of access, and density all have an influence on the lot and house components that are appropriate.

Example block component

Lot Components

Lot components such as site grading, driveway and walkway placement, and methods for entering the house give options for access. Knowing the options allows for better planning of the block and house layout.

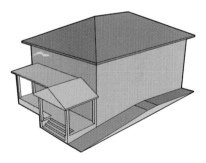

Example lot component

House Components

Knowing the necessary house components ahead of time will simplify design because it will eliminate the need to adapt a finished plan to meet certain requirements later. When the elements of the design are known from the start, it is also easier to integrate accessible features with the style of the home.

Example house component

Step 3: Assemble the Components

Select and assemble the components together in combinations that work to achieve the goals of a project and see if they work together. Use the formulas and charts provided to modify the components to fit the unique circumstances of the project.

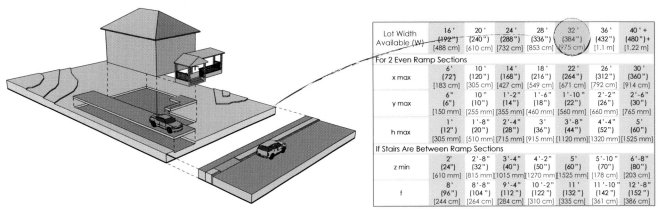

Lot Width Available (W)	16' (192") [488 cm]	20' (240") [610 cm]	24' (288") [732 cm]	28' (336") [853 cm]	32' (384") [975 cm]	36' (432") [1.1 m]	40'+ (480")+ [1.22 m]
For 2 Even Ramp Sections							
x max	6' (72') [183 cm]	10' (120") [305 cm]	14' (168") [427 cm]	18' (216") [549 cm]	22' (264") [671 cm]	26' (312") [792 cm]	30' (360") [914 cm]
y max	6" (6") [150 mm]	10" (10") [255 mm]	1'-2" (14") [355 mm]	1'-6" (18") [460 mm]	1'-10" (22") [560 mm]	2'-2" (26") [660 mm]	2'-6" (30") [765 mm]
h max	1' (12") [305 mm]	1'-8" (20") [510 mm]	2'-4" (28") [715 mm]	3' (36") [915 mm]	3'-8" (44") [1120 mm]	4'-4" (52") [1320 mm]	5' (60") [1525 mm]
If Stairs Are Between Ramp Sections							
z min	2' (24") [610 mm]	2'-8" (32") [815 mm]	3'-4" (40") [1015 mm]	4'-2" (50") [1270 mm]	5' (60") [1525 mm]	5'-10" (70") [178 cm]	6'-8" (80") [203 cm]
f	8' (96") [244 cm]	8'-8" (104") [264 cm]	9'-4" (112") [284 cm]	10'-2" (122") [310 cm]	11' (132") [335 cm]	11'-10" (142") [361 cm]	12'-8" (152") [386 cm]

Illustration of lot component assembly based on a design tool provided in the book

Step 4: Finalize the Design

Take a step back, look at the overall neighborhood pattern together with all components, and study whether the project works well in terms of character, local traditions, surrounding context, and other project goals as well as accessibility.

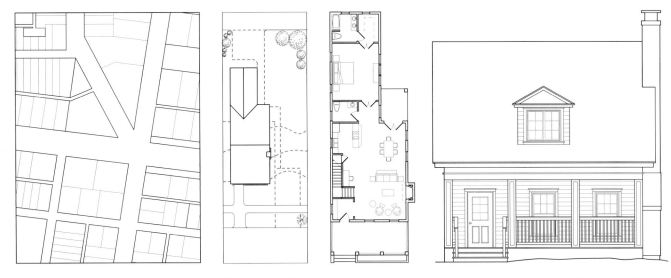

Examples of finalized block plan, lot plan, house plan, and house elevation (respectively)

SECTION 2

THE NEIGHBORLY HOUSE

A "neighborly house" is one that respects its neighbors, supports friendship formation within the block, reinforces neighborhood security, accommodates diversity, and contributes to the development of the architectural character of the neighborhood.

Sustainability

Inclusive urban housing contributes to sustainable development. The union of inclusive and sound urban design principles results in development practices that maintain a healthy social life and are environmentally friendly. Urban housing is, by its nature, more dense than sprawling suburban subdivisions and, as a result, increases social interaction opportunities. A wider range of housing options leads to more diversified and balanced populations. Higher density combined with mixed-use zoning reduces the distance residents must travel to conduct their daily activities.

Reduced travel distances also make more environmentally friendly modes of transportation than private automobiles more feasible. Walking, bicycling, and mass transit reduce the per capita emissions and fuel consumption of the community. In terms of housing construction, the goal of inclusive design is to make buildings and communities livable for all types of people. Thus, inclusive design contributes to sustainable design by reducing the need for residents to renovate existing homes or move to new ones if they become disabled, reducing use of natural resources and energy, and reducing waste. Furthermore, the reduced need to relocate maintains social networks in the neighborhood and contributes to long-term social viability and balanced neighborhood development. This is more socially sustainable than neighborhoods that accommodate only one stage of the family cycle or age group.

The most significant impact on sustainability is determined in large part by the density of development. Different house forms must be adopted to achieve higher density development. For example, in the T3 Suburban context, lots are wide and houses can stretch out across the lot to provide larger front and rear yards. Off-street parking is easy to provide, but the low density makes public transportation less viable. It is easier to provide physical accessibility, but at the same time there is reduced access to social contact opportunities. In the T4 General Urban zone, lots are narrower and the house must be long and thin to fit. The size of the front and rear yard is reduced. More limited and costlier parking options make it more difficult to provide vehicle storage next to the home, but the density levels in this zone support better public transportation service. Rowhouses and walk-up flats, which are much more energy efficient and more affordable than single-family detached dwellings, also contribute to greater social contact opportunities since

A natural recreation area in Baldwin Park, FL, promotes walking as recreation as well as providing drainage

On-grade townhouses are an inclusive and sustainable approach to housing design

Shops below apartments in Mizner Park, FL, sustain a lively street life

they provide greater proximity of neighbors and often have shared amenities like mailboxes and laundries and semi-private spaces like alleys and lobbies. But accessibility to these building types has to be planned very carefully and integrated into all design decisions, from the grading of the block to the location of entries in the dwellings. In the T5 Urban Center zone, attached housing, stacked flats, and multifamily housing are the norm, which increases sustainability still further. This zone also provides the density needed to support many neighborhood service and social spaces like fitness centers, grocery stores, and coffee shops. With three- or four-story structures, elevators and garages are more feasible. Accessibility is more easily provided since there are fewer building entries and parking is provided in separate lots and garages, or it is integrated with residential and commercial buildings.

Thus, sustainable design has a close relationship to accessibility. Access is provided in different ways to fit with the house and lot forms used at each level of density or transect zone. In the T4 zone, in particular, the design of the block, including finished grading, street, and walkway design, will play a much greater role as part of accessible design. This is not often understood. Designers tend to view the house as the focus of accessible design and neglect the block or lot. In **Sections 4 and 5**, we will demonstrate the importance of block and lot design in providing accessibility.

Marketability

The marketability of urban houses and neighborhood developments depends on many factors. Houses and lots must be the right size and price for the target markets. They must include the amenities that are expected and affordable to homebuyers in each price range. They must have an appealing style and fit with their neighbors. They also have to achieve a certain level of density to provide the urban characteristics that distinguish these developments from conventional suburban approaches. If accessible design impedes marketability, then developers and designers seeking to achieve an urban character in their projects will not embrace it. In fact, they will actively resist the incorporation of accessible features. On the other hand, suitable examples will help to counter preconceptions and demonstrate good design approaches. Examples also help convince advocates of urbanism that accessibility can contribute to meeting their goal of creating diverse communities that are inclusive and socially sustainable.

Small setbacks and raised porches in front provide a traditional character. The alleys not only provide better vehicle access, a marketable feature for all, but can also provide a no-step entry behind the houses

Social Interaction & Security

Two of the most important characteristics of neighborliness are the level of security provided and features that promote friendship formation. Research has demonstrated that when people live near each other, they are more likely to become friends because proximity leads to increased chance encounters (Michelson, 1977). The effect of proximity is moderated by personal and social factors like the need for mutual assistance and the homogeneity of the population. Certain physical features play an important role in proximity, for example, the relationship of dwellings to pedestrian routes, the location of yards, and the relationship of doors to one another. Research has also demonstrated that when privacy is hard to obtain by physical means, people use other methods to achieve it like adopting styles of public behavior that discourage social interaction. There is also evidence to indicate that security is improved when residents can easily observe people outside through windows ("eyes on the street"). Where informal surveillance is difficult, public space is often not used by residents. Territorial markers such as fences, plantings, or material changes that demarcate private from public space also contribute to increased security (Newman, 1972).

Proponents of traditional neighborhood development have proposed that an essential design feature needed to ensure social interaction and privacy in neighborhoods is the provision of "semi-private" space, especially porches or landings and a ground floor of the house raised at least 48 inches [1220 mm] above grade. Until recently, the SmartCode, one of the key tools used by TND designers, included this recommendation. TND proponents argued that the raised porch increases surveillance, provides a comfortable and secure place for outside activity, reduces unwanted privacy intrusions, encourages informal social interaction, and reduces unwanted territorial encroachments. In fact, there are many other ways to maintain privacy and security and ensure sufficient informal social contact to promote friendship formation. A larger vocabulary of forms can be used to reach the same goals without introducing barriers to accessibility. To recognize this, the SmartCode was recently amended to recognize that there are many ways to achieve these goals. This is not to say that porches and elevation changes are not relevant and important for other reasons, but they should not be viewed as the one best way to accomplish certain goals since that will reduce the range of options for providing accessibility considerably. The accompanying illustrations show several examples of other successful methods to provide privacy and security and thus support sociability in the neighborhood.

Shared semi-private space establishes territory

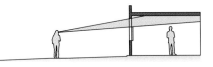

Window treatments on the lower half of windows provide privacy

Plantings provide privacy for residents

Fences establish a territorial boundary

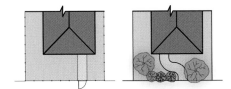

Fences & plantings create territorial control and privacy

Affordability

To ensure diversity at the community level, affordable housing for low- and moderate-income homebuyers needs to be incorporated into community development. In publicly sponsored projects like Hope VI Public Housing modernization projects, building affordable housing is the primary design goal. Nonprofit developers are sometimes the most concerned about the impact of accessible design on their mission. There are many ways to ensure affordability. In practice, every method of cost reduction possible usually must be used to control costs, including efficient space planning, careful value engineering, and selection of low-cost construction methods and details. Ultimately, the design of affordable housing leaves very little margin for adding additional features. If achieving one design goal increases costs, then total costs have to be adjusted by sacrificing another goal. Thus, affordable housing advocates are concerned that accessible design will reduce the quantity and quality of affordable housing built in a community. In particular, they fear that the addition of space to the dwelling unit or lot can add significant costs. Another concern is that viable forms of affordable housing will become impossible to build if they cannot comply with accessibility regulations, for example, small buildings with walk-up flats.

Affordable accessible housing in Decatur, GA

Affordable accessible housing in Austin, TX

While not belittling a concern for affordability, it is important to note that any new feature added to a home has the potential to add value to it. This is true with accessibility features as well as any others. For example, adding a half bath on the first-floor of a home increases its value. As long as the additional amortized cost is within the means of a homebuyer or tenant to afford, then it is an asset. However, if cost reduction measures are necessary to offset an increased cost due to accessibility, it may truly have a negative impact on quality and marketability. In this case, there will be no value added and accessibility will become a liability toward achieving affordability.

Fortunately, research and practice have demonstrated that there is no need to increase the size of a dwelling unit to provide basic accessibility. In fact, even higher levels of access can be achieved without any increase in space or negative impacts on marketability by slight modifications to plans (see, for example, Steven Winter Associates, 1993). There are few instances where adding accessibility features will not also add value, provided they are designed well. The greatest cost impact is usually related to site development – building ramps and railings to overcome steep slopes on the site. In suburban style multifamily developments, ramps and railings can be avoided by simply grading the lot carefully and setting the first-floor close to the level of the finished grade near an entryway. However, in high-density urban single-family settings with traditional house forms, accessible design can introduce some significant cost impacts in addition to marketability concerns. But, when planned at the block level, such problems can be avoided, as the reader will see in **Section 4 (Block Components)**.

Traditional Neighborhood Development

Proponents of traditional neighborhood development (TND), such as smart growth advocates and New Urbanists, promote a return to settlement patterns that have a proven history of creating livable communities and reducing urban sprawl (Ellis, 2002). They argue that we can learn what works from studying the most successful and enduring urban neighborhoods. From these studies, strategies like those incorporated into the SmartCode have been identified and incorporated into the TND design lexicon. Most early applications of TND were in new communities, often in vacation locations and rapidly developing suburban and rural areas. Critics have argued that these communities serve a population that is predominantly affluent and white and are built on "green fields" which contributes to sprawl. On the other hand, TND concepts have been used extensively in rebuilding public housing estates and in renewal of urban neighborhoods. Even more recently, TND is being combined with sustainable design in "green urbanism" (Farr, 2007). Public and private sector development policies and practices in the U.S. make it difficult to reach all the goals of TND but proponents are exploring new ideas for overcoming the barriers. Using innovative financing methods and development policies, they have developed many strategies for new development and urban redevelopment that provide a range of densities, transit oriented planning, increased housing options, flexibility in land uses, incentives for building affordable housing and accessible services, and recreation within walking distance of all residents. The popularity of walkable communities, combined with the demographic shift toward an aging society and higher gasoline prices, is increasing the popularity of TND concepts. While not all developments that espouse walkability, mixed uses, and housing choices deliver on all the goals of TND, there is clearly a change of direction underway in U.S. urban development practices that favors higher density development and mixed use land development patterns.

A walkable mixed-use housing development in Lund, Sweden, promotes traditional neighborhood values with a contemporary aesthetic

Main Street in Lady Lake, FL, promotes traditional neighborhood values with traditional building styles

TND community development plans, particularly those conceived by New Urbanists, include provision of unique facilities and landscape features to create a sense of place and an architectural character for each community that has some recognizable common physical characteristics, while still providing variety and complexity. They have not eschewed the accommodation of automobiles and big box commercial facilities, recognizing that we cannot return to an earlier era. However, they have put broader civic concerns ahead of an economic deterministic approach to urban development so that design for automobile travel takes a back seat to design for pedestrian and human powered vehicles. This urban design approach is clearly in line with inclusive design goals.

On the other hand, the emphasis on traditional housing forms in some TND projects, particularly the raised ground floor, runs counter to the goals of inclusive design because it continues the production of inaccessible housing. This book demonstrates that, by rethinking traditional house forms, designers do not have to perpetuate their problems to reap their benefits. Just as TND designers recognize that the automobile has to be accommodated in contemporary neighborhood development, the experience of disablement must also be accommodated, particularly in an aging society in which the vast majority of existing housing is inaccessible. Prior to the 1960s, people with disabilities were either cared for by family or lived in institutions. They did not have access to employment, recreation facilities, independent living services, or even polling places. So, naturally, house forms did not accommodate disability. As longevity has increased and medical science has advanced, the relevance of disability has increased. Simultaneously, the disability rights movement has brought changes to the social status of people with disabilities; it has altered our beliefs and practices about how public buildings are designed. Now we are seeing the impact in housing design. Of course, if a designer believes in a literal replication of traditional housing forms, they will always find something to critique since accessibility features were, until recently, not part of the evolution of housing forms. They have to get over this attitude or they will remain part of the problem rather than contributing to the solution and they will never truly meet the goal of creating inclusive communities.

How can the goals of inclusive housing design and traditional housing forms be reconciled? We think the answer is to incorporate inclusive design concepts in the lexicon of what may better be described as "neo-traditional" neighborhood and housing design.

This house in Kentlands at Gaithersburg, MD, is traditional in form and appearance but is a continuation of inaccessible housing production

Townhouses in Kentlands at Gaithersburg, MD, promote traditional form but do not allow universal access, forcing people who use wheelchairs to seek nontraditional housing

Luckily, there are tools for this mode of practice that can be used to integrate inclusive design principles. Form-based codes, like the SmartCode, for example, are important tools used to guide the overall design of TND developments. Form-based codes identify setbacks, or "build-to" lines, define the characteristics of streetscapes, and specify the types of buildings to be constructed in different areas. At the residential scale, advocates of TND often use pattern books to guide the development of architectural character. While pattern books do not dictate all the characteristics of houses in a community, combined with a design review process, they ensure that certain qualities will be maintained across all construction.

Thus, to aid adoption of the concepts in this book in design practice, we adopted the form of the pattern book and based our block, lot, and house designs on guidelines from the SmartCode. By grounding this book on the principles of TND and tying them to current practices, we are able to demonstrate that perceived conflicts between the goal of accessible housing design and traditional housing design concepts are reconcilable. There are solutions, just like there are solutions to the problem of automobile access and storage. The pattern book format also provides a tool for practice that is compatible with the mode of practice in the field. The ideas embodied in this book are easily transferable to other pattern books used to guide housing design in individual communities.

Neighborhood Character

Establishing neighborhood character is an important goal of urban design. The form of natural features, land uses, streets, blocks, lots, and buildings determines the overall character of a neighborhood. All these elements are interrelated, and all are important for inclusive design of communities. In this book, we will focus on the block, lot, and building (houses), but it is worth reflecting on the other elements to put this work into context.

Land use planning is particularly critical for the development of inclusive communities. Since World War II, land use practices have been dominated by a focus on segregation of specific uses (Randolph, 2003). Thus, commercial land uses are separated from residential land uses, and one type of housing is separated from another. These practices have been used almost exclusively in suburban development and also in the redevelopment of older cities. This has created barriers to accessibility for all citizens. Combined

A large highway and a business-only district divide residential neighborhoods on the Amherst-Tonawanda, NY, town line

Image courtesy of Google © 2008

with huge subsidies for road construction and free parking, this has led to great dependence on automobile transportation for daily mobility except in some inner-city urban areas in cities like New York City and San Francisco.

Segregation of housing types based on lot size restrictions and exclusive zoning for single and multifamily development has created a de facto segregation of social groups based on income and ability to obtain financing for home ownership (Fischel, 2004; Frey, 2001). In suburban development, apartments are usually walk-up garden apartments. Until the Fair Housing Amendments Act went into effect in 1991, almost all these apartments had stairs leading to them, even the first-floor units. Building an accessible single-family suburban home usually requires paying a hefty cost increase for custom features. The patterns of development and construction practices essentially limit housing opportunities for people with disabilities for economic as well as physical reasons because this group tends to have lower incomes than other groups.

The street pattern also plays an important role in inclusive design. The proliferation of major arterials with 4–6 lanes of traffic creates barriers to street crossing and makes pedestrian activity dangerous and unhealthy. Even in local neighborhoods, design features like large radius curbs, gated communities with single entries, feeder and collector streets, extensive use of cul-de-sacs, and lack of sidewalks facilitate high-speed automobile travel, increase walking distances, and create hazardous conditions for people who do not drive, including children, wheeled mobility device users, and cyclists.

This aerial view of Amherst, NY, shows the circuitous routes required to walk from one house to a neighboring house (such as A1 to B1). Note that the route from A2 to B2 requires leaving the neighborhood. This pattern isolates neighbors and reduces the sense of community

Image courtesy of Google © 2008

Perhaps the most damaging impact of the predominant form of planning today is the uniformity of urban and suburban development. Density levels are similar everywhere, and there is congestion everywhere as well. Our communities lack unique aesthetic and social neighborhood character. They are differentiated primarily by the cost of living, the quality of schools, proximity to highway interchanges, and the amenities provided in each local area, rather than by any sense of place. Even the physical details of communities are limited in variety. For example, an entire metropolitan area might have exactly the same streetscape features – sidewalk, curb, signs, lighting fixtures, etc. Choices have been reduced to a minimum, which is certainly not consistent with an inclusive design philosophy that respects and celebrates difference.

Livability & Changing Household Needs

Critics of accessibility laws often argue that these laws have a negative effect on "neighborliness." However, this perception is based on a narrow perspective on accessibility. The critics base their arguments on their own experience with modifications made to existing homes rather than experience with houses designed to be accessible from the beginning. For example, a neighbor might build a 60 foot [18 m] long switchback ramp that fills up the entire front yard in order to accommodate a child who has a severe spinal cord injury or a spouse who has epilepsy. The design of the existing house makes it difficult if not impossible to provide access any other way.

Awkward ramp added to an existing home

Even people with disabilities dislike long ugly ramps or intrusive lifts. They realize that this draws unwanted attention to a home, potentially targeting the owner as a crime victim, and creates animosity on the part of neighbors due to the resulting awkward appearance. Such a solution also reinforces the stigma of disability. However, it is important to note that traditional houses are not typically designed to support accessibility renovations; thus, they are clearly not amenable to such modifications. Such ramps are usually haphazardly designed and fit poorly with neighborhood and house character. To control costs and reduce the impact on the perceived value of a property, they are often built in a temporary manner so that they can be removed when no longer needed. They are usually constructed without professional design assistance and with little thought to aesthetics. Even where care is taken to build a beautiful structure, making adaptations for accessibility may require a heroic effort. This does not mean, however, that accessibility cannot be achieved while still maintaining neighborliness. In particular, if the home is designed to have an accessible entry from the start, awkward modifications should never be needed.

Dangerous condition created by using a series of temporary ramps

Existing publications on accessible design contribute to the belief that accessibility is not compatible with neighborliness because they illustrate only a limited number of options for housing design and tend to include many houses that have a clinical or institutional appearance because they are designed for individuals with disabilities. To the authors' knowledge, no book has ever addressed traditional neighborhood and house design in an urban context or attempted to demonstrate how accessibility can respond to contextual issues.

"Heroic effort" required to make a house accessible

When presented with examples of new suburban housing that is accessible, urban designers argue that suburban examples are not applicable to urban contexts. And, in fact, the examples illustrated in manuals and books are almost exclusively based on suburban single-family detached home models on large lots, garden apartments in large complexes, or high-rise apartment buildings. In these examples, conditions are ideal for providing accessibility. The architectural character is not seriously affected because, in most cases, the examples used do not have a character based on a carefully worked out architectural language. Often the examples in manuals are simply diagrammatic. In other words, the examples used imply that there is no problem providing accessibility because they have been selected to make it look easy or treat accessibility as a purely functional concern. Since the building types illustrated in the manuals are very limited, urban design critics argue that if these are the only types of units that can be constructed and still comply with the law, it will seriously limit the ability to develop urban neighborhoods with a diverse array of housing types and a meaningful architectural character. This, they argue, will limit the social diversity of neighborhoods and thus reinforce conventional planning practices that lead to sprawl and social segregation.

Suburban homes like this one in Bolingbrook, IL, are ideal for providing on-grade access because the lot is large and can easily be graded

In an inclusive design approach, accessible design should embrace neighborliness and reinforce it, not work against it. Thus, methods used to achieve access to houses in traditional neighborhood developments must consider many other design goals. It is not enough for designers and builders to copy details and diagrams from technical manuals when they need to provide accessible dwelling units. They have to treat accessibility as an integrated part of creating livable homes and communities. Otherwise, they perpetuate stereotypes and abrogate their responsibilities for good design in general.

An on-grade front entry is provided without noticeable difference from typical suburban practices (Bolingbrook, IL)

SECTION 3

LEVELS OF ACCESS

This section describes how inclusive housing contributes to livability. The section begins with a history of accessible housing policy to put current ideas into perspective. A rationale is provided for creating different levels of access in the housing stock. Information on costs is provided to demonstrate how much value is obtained by incorporating inclusive design features.

Short History of Accessible Housing

Starting in the mid-1960s, accessible housing policies in the U.S. were developed to ensure that a fixed percentage of units, roughly equal to the percentage of people with severe disabilities in the adult population, incorporated accessibility features. This approach was only applied to publicly subsidized construction and is still mandated by the Architectural Barriers Act, Section 504 of the Rehabilitation Act, and Title II of the Americans with Disabilities Act (http://www.access-board.gov/, http://www.ada.gov/reg3a .html, http://www.fairhousingfirst.org/). These laws require 5% of the units in buildings that are covered by these acts to be fully accessible, including an accessible path of travel to and inside the unit, wider doors, the installation of grab bars, roll-in shower stalls, lower counters and cabinets, knee clearances, and higher toilets, among other features. It is these laws that mandate accessibility to 5% of the units in public housing modernization and reconstruction programs like Hope VI and similar public financing programs. Many states adopted laws that mirrored the federal laws or added additional requirements for public and, in some cases, privately developed housing.

Accessible houses in a Hope VI low-income housing project at Oak Hill in Pittsburgh, PA

By the late 1970s, policymakers realized that not everyone with a disability could be accommodated by the 5% set aside policy. Experience with that approach revealed that accessibility is only one of many factors that determine where an individual might want to live. An accessible unit in a building that is not served well by public transportation, for example, is not a desirable place for a person with a mobility disability to live if they cannot or do not drive. Federal programs that subsidized construction, like Section 202, produced many new buildings with the 5% set aside. However, most of these buildings are restricted to older residents. The only younger residents allowed are people with disabilities. These buildings are not desirable for young adults who want to live near their peers, and they sometimes create conflicts between the younger and older tenants due to lifestyle and generational differences. Other limitations of the set aside policy are that publicly assisted housing is not available everywhere, not everyone qualifies for subsidized buildings, and the sizes of the available apartments do not always meet the needs of people who are looking for accessible housing. Furthermore, landlords cannot be expected to hold an accessible unit off the market indefinitely. Once an accessible unit is rented, often not to a person with a disability, it is effectively not available to someone who may need it. Finally, these units are designed with all the accessibility features built in. But not every person with a disability has the same needs. Some wheelchair users can stand up and others cannot. Some cook and some do not. Some have sensory rather than mobility impairments. The best example of different needs is the height of toilets. The typical toilet seat is 15 to 16 inches [380–405 mm] high while the accessible toilet seat is 17 to 19 inches [430–480 mm] high. Anyone of short stature who does not use a wheelchair and has used an accessible toilet has had direct experience with this problem.

In response to the limitations of the set aside approach, in the 1970s, a new concept emerged in the U.S. based on a practice adopted in northern Europe called "adaptable housing." A survey of 200 people with disabilities in the U.S. confirmed the assumptions behind this concept (Steinfeld, Schroeder, and Bishop, 1979; Bostrom, Corning, Mace, and Long, 1987). This approach to accessible housing includes fewer accessibility features but applies them on a broader basis. Adaptable housing includes basic access features such as minimum wheelchair clearances to avoid the need for expensive renovations in the future. Other features are included that make it easy to increase the accessibility of the unit if needed, for example, reinforced walls for future installation of grab bars and kitchen cabinets designed in a way that will facilitate adaptation to wheelchair use. If necessary, a higher level of access can be provided very easily and inexpensively. This idea was incorporated into the revisions to the ANSI A117.1 Standard in 1980, and a simplified version was later incorporated into the Fair Housing Act that was implemented starting in 1991. This act covers all multifamily buildings (more than three units) whether publicly or privately financed. According to this law, all units in elevator-equipped buildings and all ground floor units in walk-up buildings must be adaptable, and similar provisions to public building access are required in all the common or public spaces of multifamily projects. The adaptability features are only noticeable to the knowledgeable observer (SWA, 1993). Adaptable units can be incorporated on a widespread basis and do not have to be reserved for people with disabilities. It is important to note that adaptable housing does not substitute for the 5% set aside units. It provides more choices and opportunities, but there are many people with severe disabilities who need the additional features of accessible units to live independently.

Multifamily building designed to meet the Fair Housing Act in Boston, MA

Depending on the region, 60–70 percent of Americans live in single-family housing, and the vast majority of these are in the private sector (U.S. Census Bureau, 2001). Only a very small number of single-family units currently are covered by existing accessibility regulations – the 5% set aside in publicly financed projects. So people who want an accessible single-family home are effectively relegated to building a custom home or making extensive renovations to an existing home. Builders generally charge a stiff premium to add accessibility features to a new home or make accessible renovations. Moreover, it is difficult to find knowledgeable designers and builders who can design accessible housing properly. Disability advocates argue that this situation amounts to de facto discrimination in housing. Finally, a lot of housing is very difficult if not impossible to make accessible. To address this situation, a new approach to accessible housing called "Visitability" was developed and is spreading rapidly across the country as a means to provide limited access features in single-family housing.

Visitability

Visitability is an affordable, sustainable, and accessible design approach that specifically targets single-family homes (including buildings with 2–3 units that are not covered by the Fair Housing Act). The movement for basic access in all new homes was initiated in the United States in 1987 by disability rights advocate Eleanor Smith and her advocacy group, Concrete Change. They adopted the term "Visitability" in 1990 upon learning that advocates in Great Britain used the term for a similar concept. A Visitable home is intended to be a residence for anyone and to provide access to everyone. Visitability strives to provide a baseline level of accessibility in all new home construction, in hopes of benefiting the entire population. A Visitable home has these features: one no-step entrance, low thresholds, doorways that provide 32 inches [815 mm] of clearance, hallways with 36 inch [915 mm] clear width, basic access to at least a half bath on the main floor, reinforcement in walls next to toilets for future installation of grab bars if they are needed, and light switches and electrical outlets within comfortable reach for all. See Table 3-1 and Appendix A for a more comprehensive list of these features and for references to more specific design guides.

These features are considered the most essential for a person with mobility impairments to visit or live in a home, at least temporarily. As of January 2008, 57 state and local municipalities had either a voluntary or a mandatory Visitability program in place (Maisel, Smith, and Steinfeld, 2008). Currently, most of these programs apply only to single-family housing built with public support. Depending on the locality, this could mean use of publicly owned land, as in many Habitat for Humanity projects, waivers of fees, cash grants, tax credits, and other forms of direct or in-kind public support. A federal law is under development that would apply to all single-family construction that receives federal assistance. At the time this book was written, two local governments – those of Bolingbrook, IL, and Pima County, AZ – had adopted visitability ordinances that apply to all single-family housing, including privately funded buildings.

Basic Visitability Features	For more info...
▶ One no-step entry that can be at the front, side, rear, or through a garage	Pages 51–56
▶ ¼–½ in. [6.4–13 mm] thresholds	Page 66
▶ Doorways have at least a 32 in. [815 mm] wide clear opening	Page 63
▶ Hallways are 36 in. [915 mm] clear minimum	Page 74
▶ Basic access to at least a half bath on the main floor	Pages 79 & 80
▶ Reinforced walls at toilets for future installation of grab bars	Pages 79 & 80
▶ Light switches and electrical outlets 15–48 in. [380–1220 mm] from finished floor	Page 63

Table 3-1

As Visitability has spread around the country, many different interpretations have emerged as local and state governments have reinterpreted the requirements. Since most of the laws do not provide detailed criteria for the Visitable features, there has been some confusion over what the requirements of the laws really entail. The ICC/ANSI A117.1 Standard on Accessible and Usable Buildings and Facilities is the consensus standard in the U.S. for defining the details of accessible construction. This standard is referenced by model building codes like the ICC Code and state accessibility laws. The standards used for the 5% set aside units are incorporated in that standard as Type A Units.

The Fair Housing requirements are incorporated as Type B Units. In the latest version of the standard, the committee approved the addition of a section on Type C (Visitable) Units, which is intended for use in defining the technical requirements of Visitability. This standard will be helpful in clarifying the requirements and creating uniformity as new laws are passed. In Appendix A we have included a summary of the Type C (Visitable) requirements to assist designers in understanding them.

Since the standards are developed for use in a legal context, they include many provisions that heretofore have not been included in Visitability laws to address potential problems with enforcement. For example, one of the issues that needed to be addressed was what resources in the home have to be on the accessible level. The committee concluded that the goal of Visitability is to provide access for a short time and to as wide a range of units as possible. Thus, at a minimum, accessibility is required to at least a 120 square foot [11 m^2] living space, a half or full bathroom, and a food preparation facility. The latter does not have to be a full kitchen.

On one hand, these requirements preclude dwelling unit designs that have a garage occupying all of the first-floor. On the other, they could fall short of providing a home that is truly livable for a person who cannot climb stairs. Local governments can provide exceptions to the application of these standards. For example, they could exempt houses built on flood plains where the first-floor of the home has to be located higher than four feet above grade. They could exempt freestanding carriage houses. In addition, they could exempt apartments above stores, as long as there are fewer than four apartments in the building. Otherwise, the Fair Housing Act comes into play.

From a traditional neighborhood development perspective, the requirements of the standard provide a great deal of freedom and are reasonable. They are even amenable to building types like live-work lofts and rowhouses that have a kitchen, dining, and formal living rooms on a second-floor. Because they do not require accessibility to all units in a 2–3 unit building, walk-up apartments above a garage are acceptable if the main house is Visitable. It should be noted that single-family unit types where the garage occupies the entire first-floor of a building are not very desirable in traditional neighborhood developments, or, for that matter, in any neighborhood, because they make the streetscape a solid wall of garages and divorce the living floors from the yard or street.

A fundamental principle of Visitability is that through good design, basic accessibility to single-family housing can be provided in most cases with a minimal financial cost. In other words, the limited list of features is so inexpensive that the concept can be applied on a universal basis. The professional construction cost estimator hired by the government of Pima County, AZ, estimated the total additional cost at about $100 for new houses built on a concrete slab (which included a no-step entrance, 30 inch [760 mm] clear interior doors, lever handles, and reinforcement in bathroom walls), and this included $25 in overhead and profit for the builder (Williams and Altaffer, 2000). Ed Phillips, executive director of the Homebuilders Association of Georgia, confirmed this estimate: "When Visitability features are planned in advance by a well-informed builder, [the] typical added cost is very low for a new, single-family detached home…less than $100 for homes on concrete slabs, and $300–600 for homes with crawl spaces or basements" (Concrete Change, 2004). Moreover, the few studies that have actually analyzed the specific costs associated with Visitability confirm that introducing its features through retrofitting results in significantly higher costs. The Center for Inclusive Design and Environmental Access asked two construction managers to estimate the cost of Visitability features for a small house built with a full basement. They confirmed the low cost impact (see Table 3-2).

	New Construction	Solution
No-Step Entry	No cost	• Site graded up toward rear • 6 ft [1830 mm] ramp to wooden deck at rear • Credit for stairs
Widen Interior Doors	$25	• $5 more per door
Expanded Bathroom	No cost	• Shaved 10 ft² [1 m²] from living-dining area

Table 3-2

One common misconception associated with the costs of Visitability is that wider doors are not readily available and are more expensive. This misconception may be because few retail home improvement stores stock the 34 inch [865 mm] door that is necessary for a 32 inch [815 mm] clear width door opening. Home improvement stores stock only the products in demand by their customers. Since home improvements are made to older homes, there is no demand for 34 inch [865 mm] doors, because the existing housing stock has, at present, very few doors of that size. However, builders of new homes purchase their doors from wholesalers, not home improvement stores. When purchased in bulk, large builders report that the cost of 34 inch [865 mm] or 36 inch [915 mm] doors is practically identical to narrower doors. The IDeA Center confirmed this by surveying five wholesale suppliers across the U.S. (see Table 3-3).

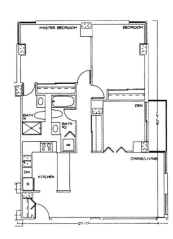

Example plan before Visitability changes (from "The Cost of Accessible Housing")

Available/Cost of Interior Single Prehung Doors (IDeA, 2006)				
No casing, hollow core, 4⁹⁄₁₆ in. jamb, dull brass hinges, 6 panel				
City	In Stock?	32 in. cost [815 mm]	34 in. cost [865 mm]	36 in. cost [915 mm]
Boston, MA	Yes	$70.45	$72.95	$72.95
Chicago, IL	Yes	$58.46	$59.98	$63.36
San Diego, CA	Yes	$73.13	$74.29	$76.50
Portland, OR	Yes	$68.83	$69.93	$72.53
Dallas, TX	Yes	$56.63	$56.89	$59.35

Table 3-3

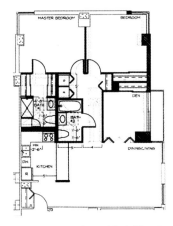

Example plan after Visitability changes (from "The Cost of Accessible Housing")

Another misconception is that providing accessibility to the interior of the unit adds space to the overall house and thus increases its cost. A research study sponsored by the U.S. Department of Housing and Urban Development on the impact of the Fair Housing Act Accessibility Guidelines demonstrated that this is not the case (Steven Winter Associates, 2001). This study was the most detailed study ever completed on the cost of accessible housing. Nine existing housing developments and more than thirty dwelling units were redesigned to meet both the FHAAG and the ANSI A117.1 (1986) standard. A wide range of different multifamily housing types was included. It was still possible to redesign all the units to meet both standards without sacrificing marketability or increasing their size. The cost impact was estimated by the developers themselves. The results showed that the marginal cost increase was less than 1% of total development costs. Although this study focused only on multifamily housing, the examples illustrated in the book demonstrate that accessibility is easily achieved even in small dwellings. Another example is the redesign of "Katrina Cottage" emergency housing for people displaced by Hurricane Katrina. In our experience, there are very few house plans that cannot easily be designed to include the Visitability features. It is important to note that Visitability can also add value to a home. These benefits extend to the entire population, not just people with disabilities. Visitability can have a positive impact on safety, aesthetics, livability, long-term maintenance, resale, and other factors (Maisel, Smith, and Steinfeld, 2008).

Lifespan Housing

The newest innovation in accessible housing is design for aging in place or "Lifespan housing." Survey research studies consistently indicate that older people prefer to stay in their own homes rather than move to accommodate age-related housing and care needs. The current generation of older people is more aware of their potential future needs. For example, a national survey of buyers over the age of 50 conducted by the National Association of Home Builders found that 70% of the respondents preferred single-story homes (Wylde, 2002). Design for aging in place should include a broader range of features than adaptable housing. In particular, designs for sensory limitations, security, and the prevention of falls are key goals. Moreover, community context is also important. Aging in place, with any decent level of quality of life, requires livable neighborhoods that have conveniently located community services, opportunities for recreation and work nearby, a vibrant street life, and informal gathering places through which neighbors can more easily get to know each other.

There is a tendency to view design for aging in place as something desirable only by people over the age of 50. However, the same features that assist older residents to age gracefully in their homes and neighborhoods are also desirable for other age groups. Stress on families due to an increase in single headed households, a need for both parents to work during child-rearing years, time demands of competitive work environments, the concern for safety and security of children, rising rates of asthma, and the health effects of inactive lifestyles all contribute to the desirability of safe, convenient, and healthy housing and neighborhoods.

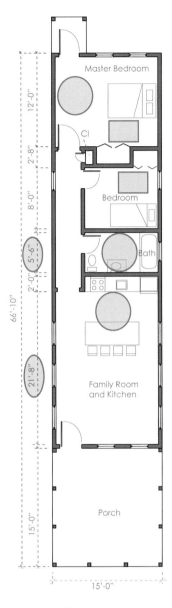

Modified Katrina Cottage
Original design by
Mississippi Renewal Housing
Designs; Erika Albright and
Matthew Lister

If we generalize the concept of design for aging in place, we can see that it has some key benefits at each stage of the lifespan—safety and security for children, stress reduction for parents, and support for aging in place for older residents. So the term "Lifespan housing" applies to the entire lifespan, not just the later years. Nevertheless, today, the most important market for such housing is the older generation. The size of the population over the age of 65 will increase from about 12% in 2004 to about 20% by the year 2030 (U.S. Census Bureau, 2004). This market includes early retirees and "empty nesters" who hope to move to a new home and age in place for the rest of their lives. If we include everyone over the age of 50, it includes about 25% of the current U.S. population! It is important to note that few older people desire to live in age-restricted communities. As the Boomers age, demand will likely increase for such communities simply because there are so many more Boomers as compared to previous older generations. However, the majority of buyers over the age of 50 are not interested in those communities.

Although the features of the other types of accessible housing have been codified by various laws and the ICC/ANSI A117.1 Standard, there has not been a codification of Lifespan design housing. Our interpretation of the concept includes "essential" and "optional" features.

Essential Lifespan Features	For more info...
▶ One no-step path to a no-step entry that can be at the front, side, rear, or through a garage (¼–½ in. [6.4–13 mm] thresholds)	Page 66 (thresholds)
▶ No step access to patios, balconies, and terraces (¼–½ in. [6.4–13 mm] thresholds)	Page 66 (thresholds)
▶ Doorways have at least a 34 in. [865 mm] wide clear opening with appropriate approach clearances	Pages 63–65
▶ Door handles are 34–38 inches [865–965 mm] from the floor	Page 66
▶ Hallways and passageways are 42 in. [1065 mm] clear minimum	Page 74
▶ Access to at least one full bath on the main floor with reinforced walls at toilets and tubs for the future installation of grab bars	Pages 81–82
▶ Cabinetry in kitchen that allows a person to work in a seated position	Pages 84–85

Table 3-4

Essential Lifespan Features (cont'd)	For more info...
▶ Light switches and electrical outlets 24–48 in. [610–1220 mm] from finished floor	Page 63
▶ Stairways have tread widths at least 11 in. [280 mm] deep and risers no greater than 7 in. [180 mm] high	Pages 68–72
▶ Good lighting throughout the house including task lighting in critical locations (e.g. under kitchen cabinets)	
▶ Non-glare surfaces	
▶ Contrasting colors to promote good perception of edges and boundaries	
▶ Clear floor space of at least 30 x 48 in. [760 x 1220 mm] in front of all appliances, fixtures, and cabinetry	Page 62
▶ Front-loading laundry equipment	
▶ Ample kitchen and closet storage or adjustable shelving within 28–48 in. [710–1220 mm]	Pages 83–87
▶ Comfortable reach zones	Page 63

Table 3-5

Optional Lifespan Features (partial list)	For more info...
▶ No steps on path toward any entry	
▶ One-story plan, or residential elevator, or stacked closets and framed-out ceiling/floor to allow future installation of a residential elevator	
▶ Adjustable height kitchen/bathroom sinks	Pages 84–85
▶ Appliances with built-in convenience features (e.g. side-by-side refrigerator with water and ice access in door)	
▶ Cabinets with built-in convenience features (e.g. full extension sliding drawers and shelves)	Page 83
▶ Intercoms in every room and major entries	
▶ Smart house system	

Table 3-6

Inclusive Design

Visitable and Lifespan housing are examples of a design philosophy called "inclusive design" (often referred to as "universal design"). Unlike the 5% set aside of accessible units, these design concepts can be applied to all houses, not just a small number reserved for a protected class of individuals. The goal of inclusive design is to increase usability, safety, and health for a diverse population. It provides benefits to everyone by making the physical environment more usable, for a broader range of people, in more situations. Examples of inclusive design include utensils that have wide, soft, non-slip handles, low floor buses with ramps, closed captioning built into all televisions, and public buildings and facilities that are especially enabling for a wide array of users.

The Detroit Metro Airport has three circulation systems to provide choices and speed when needed

By producing an environment that is more inclusive, there will be less need for specific accommodations for people with disabilities. Moreover, the benefits for all will generate a larger constituency to support the provision of increased usability. Inclusive design proponents argue that if this new paradigm is widely adopted, people without disabilities will become more effective advocates for improving access for those who do have disabilities. They also believe that the practice of inclusive design will lead to greater social integration of people with disabilities, which will address the ultimate goal of social participation in work, recreation, and civic life more effectively than accessible design.

Some critics of accessible design argue that by designing for the "lowest common denominator," the majority of building users receive fewer benefits. For example, adding space for wheelchair use in a bathroom can make it more difficult for a person who holds on to supporting surfaces and devices while moving from fixture to fixture. Accessibility laws target a limited group of beneficiaries and focus on eliminating discrimination. Inclusive design has a broader audience. A true inclusive design should benefit everyone. For example, the design of a large bathroom can provide supportive surfaces and devices within reach at all times. It is important to note that many accessibility features are great examples of inclusive design. For instance, curb ramps were originally added to streetscapes to allow wheelchair users to have safe access to sidewalks. However, it soon became obvious that curb ramps benefit parents with strollers, shoppers with carts, travelers with rolling luggage, bicyclists, skaters, frail older people, and small children. Who climbs the curb when they can use the curb ramp next to it?

The interior ramp at the Rose Planetarium in New York exposes the exhibits to all visitors

A misconception about inclusive design is that it is idealistic and not practical to accommodate everyone who may use a product or building. It is true that it may be impossible to accommodate everyone, especially if the goal is full independent use. However, inclusive design should not be viewed as an absolute. The term inclusive "designing" is more appropriate. While accessibility codes determine the bottom line, they are only minimum requirements. Inclusive design is contextual and evolutionary. The idea is to strive constantly for a higher level of usability for a broader and broader range of people. Like sustainable design, there is always another level of performance to reach.

The accessible entry at the Beacon House at Beacon Hill in Boston is an example of how inclusive design can be provided to historic buildings with style and grace

Another common misconception of inclusive design is that it will reduce the positive aesthetic impact of a design and thus lessen its value to the majority. However, aesthetics should play an important role in inclusive design. The emotional aspect of design is clearly as important as the functional aspect. In fact, the two are closely related. Research demonstrates that a positive emotional response to a design can override negative functional characteristics and good functional characteristics contribute to a positive emotional response (Norman, 2004).

Emotional responses occur at three different levels of experience – the visceral, the behavioral, and the reflective (Norman, 2004). People like traditional neighborhoods and housing for all three reasons. First, traditional neighborhoods and houses provide a complex multi-sensory experience that is very appealing to the general population at the visceral level because, unlike monotonous and uniform suburban sprawl, traditional forms are stimulating, surprising at every turn, and rich in levels of detail. Second, as the TND proponents argue, traditional forms have evolved over centuries to promote access to services, security, privacy, and social interaction – key behavioral goals for all residents. Third, traditional forms have a connotation of high value due to their association with historic places and high status like Beacon Hill in Boston, MA, or Georgetown in Washington, DC. So, at the reflective level, they have high appeal. As long as inclusive design does not negatively detract from those connotations, it should bring additional positive emotional benefits to traditional design because it directly addresses the visceral and behavioral levels of emotion. A street that is more convenient and safer to use for a wide range of individuals will clearly produce a more positive emotional response.

A ramp added to social space in the Beacon House is an example of how inclusive design can be integrated without being overtly noticeable

Several years ago, our research team tested four different bathroom designs with wheelchair users and people without disabilities: one that was not accessible at all, one that met the Fair Housing rules, one that met the Type A dwelling rules, and one that had larger clearances and fixtures and accessories that provided even more convenience (inclusive design). While the wheelchair users benefited progressively more from the second, third, and fourth designs, the able-bodied group only benefited from the inclusive design. Moreover, both groups rated the inclusive design significantly better than the others (Steinfeld and Danford, 1999). This example demonstrates that people with disabilities are more sensitive to problematic aspects of environments and products and thus benefit in more obvious ways. But a higher level of convenience is necessary to benefit an able-bodied population. That added convenience for all, of course, will benefit people with disabilities even more than the minimal improvements in codes. This is what inclusive design is all about.

SECTION 4

BLOCK COMPONENTS

This section of the book describes the components that support inclusive design within a block. It illustrates different block layouts and includes recommendations on how to combine them to create a desired outcome. Block types that are typically used in different transect zones are described, including benefits and detriments of each with regard to inclusive design. Solutions for topography are provided as well as guidelines for good intersection design and pedestrian circulation.

Overview

This section presents some common prototype block plans and evaluates the accessibility of each. Consult this section when laying out a new neighborhood. It can also be useful for identifying the limitations of existing block patterns. By knowing those limitations, it may be possible to introduce design elements that can alleviate them. Consider the relationship of each block to the rest of the neighborhood.

Neighborhood Design

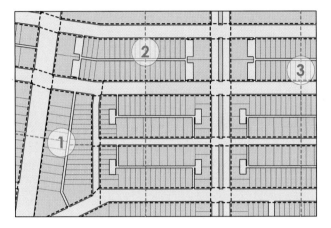

Block-to-Block Access

Connectivity for everyone to everywhere should be the test for effective planning at this scale.

In this example, a network of pedestrian paths is shown. Pedestrian short cuts across blocks will cut down travel time and increase opportunities for social interaction with neighbors.

▶ Street crossings and public transportation stops should facilitate access and use by people with a wide range of functional limitations.

▶ Provide pedestrian paths that reduce distances to neighborhood resources, e.g. paths that cut across blocks **(1–3)**.

▶ Site furniture such as benches, seating walls, bus shelters, and lighting should support a wide range of needs and be located to support social interaction.

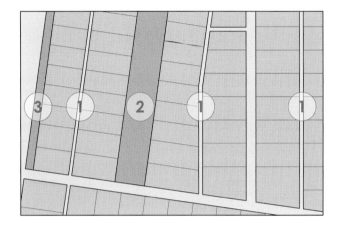

Lot Planning

Lots should provide more accessibility and safety for all residents.

This example demonstrates how a few blocks can be arranged to provide choices in accessible lot configurations.

▶ Accessible paths of travel should connect buildings and site amenities to all related adjoining uses.

▶ Alleys **(1)** reduce curb cuts required for driveways and make sidewalks safer and more pleasant.

▶ Mews **(2)** and parkway strips **(3)** provide vehicle-free zones and safe recreation areas immediately next to houses.

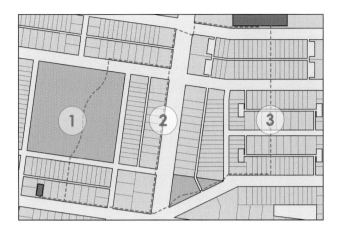

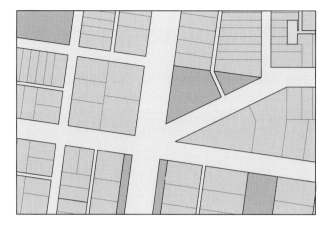

Proximity to Services

Providing continuity of access for a diverse public is fundamental to ensuring access to services and amenities for everyone.

In the figure above, there are three possible paths from the highlighted house to a local service site. The first is a more scenic route **(1)**, the second runs along main roads only **(2)**, and the third is a combination of scenic, roadside, and shortcut routes **(3)**.

▶ Street planning should provide options and choices for access to community resources for everyone.

▶ Communities should have different types of transportation access and options.

▶ Recreation and leisure resources should accommodate local cultural traditions.

▶ Pathways should not have dead-ends or unexpected staircases without an alternative accessible route.

▶ Locating schools and churches on main roads rather than embedding them deep in neighborhoods will reduce traffic in residential areas.

Social Integration

The opportunity for neighborhood social integration for all residents should be facilitated and supported by planning decisions.

Centrally located green spaces promote social interaction and outdoor recreation.

In this example, there are five different lot widths, all close to each other, and different types of green space.

▶ Provide sufficient variety in housing types to accommodate a wide range of households and living arrangements. Variety in lot size can ensure that there will be variety in house types.

▶ Safe, secure, and accessible sidewalks and other pedestrian paths should support active living for all residents.

▶ Provide social interaction opportunities for all age groups at the neighborhood level. These opportunities should take advantage of natural meeting places like the intersection of paths and the location of playgrounds.

Block Layout

Block components include streets, alleys, intersections, walkways, and parking lots. The lot sizes, the types of pedestrian and vehicular circulation, and the parking options determine the accessibility of blocks. Considering inclusive design when planning a block will make it easier to plan accessibility to each lot and enable accessible housing to be built on any lot. Depending on the topography, there may be some lots that have limited or no accessibility. Every single block layout has some limitations since there are competing design goals. In the accompanying illustrations, we provide evaluations of typical block layouts from an accessible and inclusive design perspective. Walkways are not shown in the block illustrations due to the small scale but are illustrated on pages 44–47. The drawing below references the different block layouts organized by transect zone.

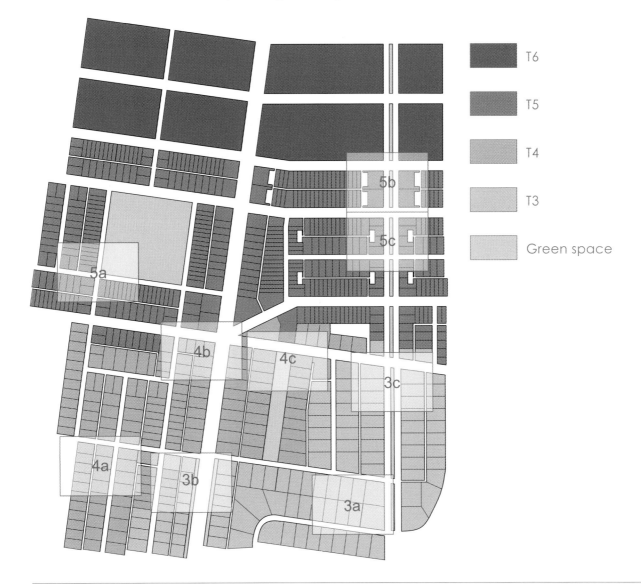

T6

T5

T4

T3

Green space

Transect 3 Block Layout

Large lots with single-family detached homes are typical of T3 blocks. Each lot has a generous yard and parking for at least two cars. Parking can be provided on streets as well as in driveways, garages, and alleys. The blocks in this transect are long and narrow with streets that are more suited to vehicular than pedestrian traffic.

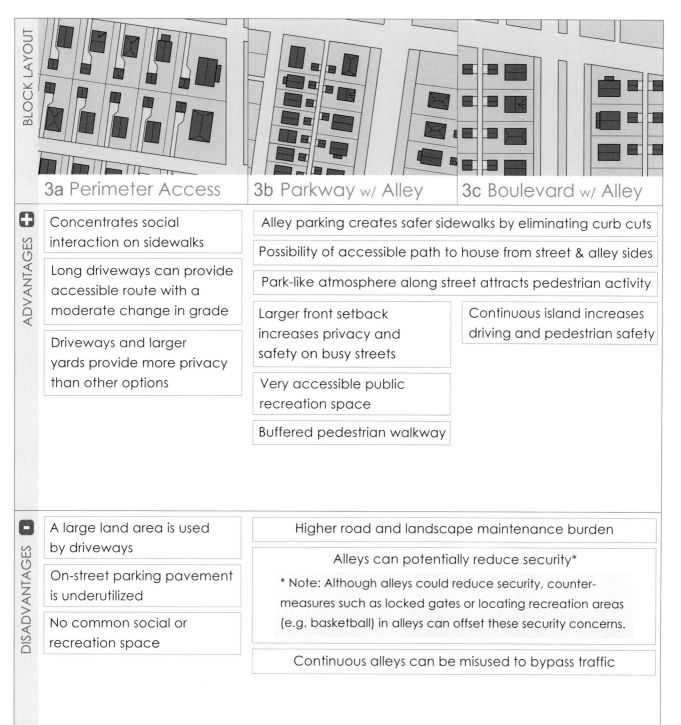

BLOCK LAYOUT

3a Perimeter Access | 3b Parkway w/ Alley | 3c Boulevard w/ Alley

ADVANTAGES

Concentrates social interaction on sidewalks

Long driveways can provide accessible route with a moderate change in grade

Driveways and larger yards provide more privacy than other options

Alley parking creates safer sidewalks by eliminating curb cuts

Possibility of accessible path to house from street & alley sides

Park-like atmosphere along street attracts pedestrian activity

Larger front setback increases privacy and safety on busy streets

Continuous island increases driving and pedestrian safety

Very accessible public recreation space

Buffered pedestrian walkway

DISADVANTAGES

A large land area is used by driveways

On-street parking pavement is underutilized

No common social or recreation space

Higher road and landscape maintenance burden

Alleys can potentially reduce security*

* Note: Although alleys could reduce security, counter-measures such as locked gates or locating recreation areas (e.g. basketball) in alleys can offset these security concerns.

Continuous alleys can be misused to bypass traffic

Transect 4 Block Layout

These blocks feature medium-sized lots for single-family homes that may be detached, semi-detached, townhouses, or rowhouses. Parking is available for each unit by parking pad, garage, or small lots, all accessed from alleys. On-street parking is available as well. T4 blocks are shorter than in the T3 zone, and they support pedestrian as well as vehicular traffic.

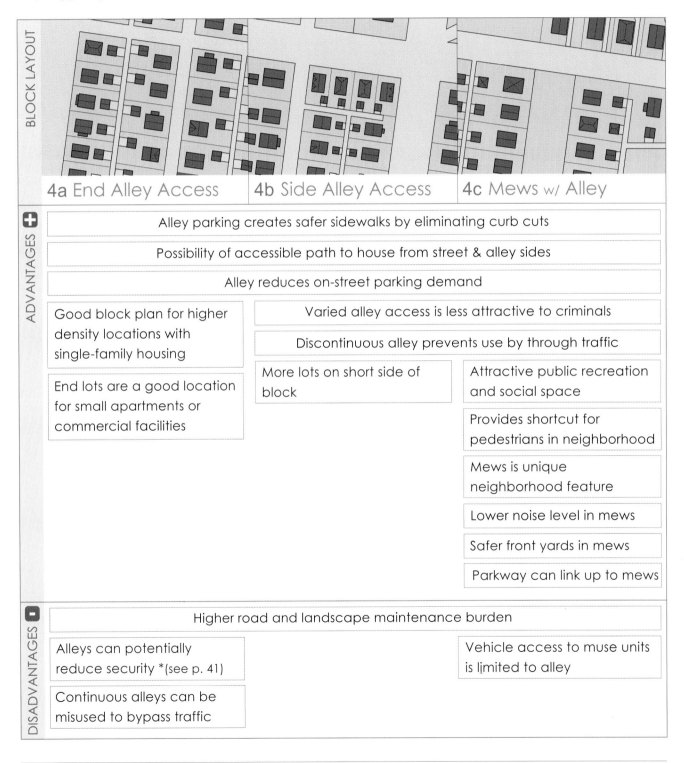

BLOCK LAYOUT

| 4a End Alley Access | 4b Side Alley Access | 4c Mews w/ Alley |

ADVANTAGES

Alley parking creates safer sidewalks by eliminating curb cuts

Possibility of accessible path to house from street & alley sides

Alley reduces on-street parking demand

Good block plan for higher density locations with single-family housing	Varied alley access is less attractive to criminals	
	Discontinuous alley prevents use by through traffic	
End lots are a good location for small apartments or commercial facilities	More lots on short side of block	Attractive public recreation and social space
		Provides shortcut for pedestrians in neighborhood
		Mews is unique neighborhood feature
		Lower noise level in mews
		Safer front yards in mews
		Parkway can link up to mews

DISADVANTAGES

Higher road and landscape maintenance burden

Alleys can potentially reduce security *(see p. 41)		Vehicle access to muse units is limited to alley
Continuous alleys can be misused to bypass traffic		

Transect 5 Block Layout

Blocks in this transect are composed of small, narrow lots with minimal yards. A variety of housing types may be used here: single-family attached on narrow lots, semi-detached homes, as well as small apartment buildings. Off-street parking is available for just one car per unit in a shared garage, driveway, or lot. Neighborhood garages or lots can be included to provide additional parking.

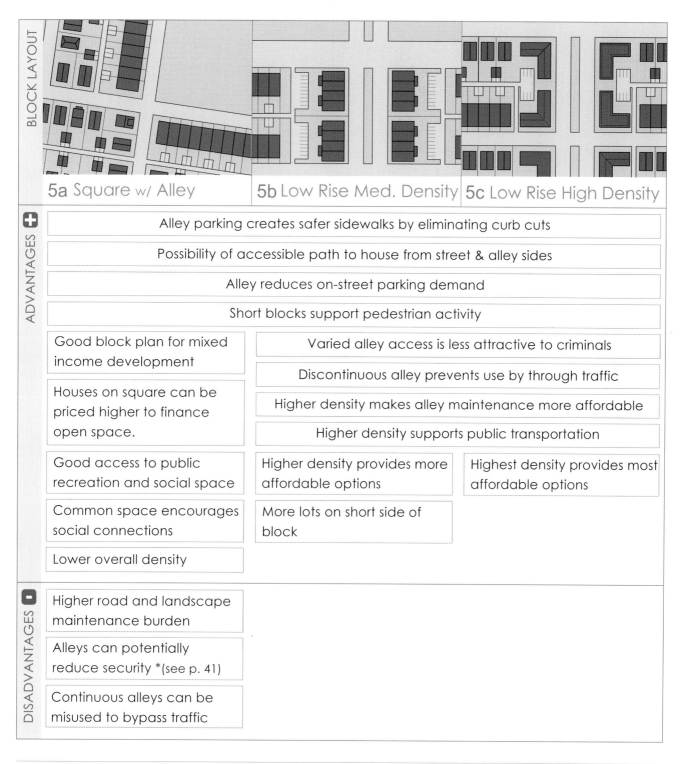

BLOCK LAYOUT

5a Square w/ Alley | **5b** Low Rise Med. Density | **5c** Low Rise High Density

ADVANTAGES

Alley parking creates safer sidewalks by eliminating curb cuts

Possibility of accessible path to house from street & alley sides

Alley reduces on-street parking demand

Short blocks support pedestrian activity

Good block plan for mixed income development	Varied alley access is less attractive to criminals
	Discontinuous alley prevents use by through traffic
Houses on square can be priced higher to finance open space.	Higher density makes alley maintenance more affordable
	Higher density supports public transportation
Good access to public recreation and social space	Higher density provides more affordable options · Highest density provides most affordable options
Common space encourages social connections	More lots on short side of block
Lower overall density	

DISADVANTAGES

Higher road and landscape maintenance burden

Alleys can potentially reduce security *(see p. 41)

Continuous alleys can be misused to bypass traffic

Intersections & Walkways

Intersections and walkways are important block components for inclusive design. If not properly designed, they can be hazardous and inconvenient. Two key design issues are the safe detection of edges and the construction of smooth, even walking and rolling surfaces. The best solutions are often the simplest. This section discusses these simple solutions and shows examples of their implementation. This section also shows a construction detail of a properly constructed curb ramp on page 46.

The ability to detect the edges between pedestrian and vehicle areas is an important safety consideration for all pedestrians and a critical feature for people with vision and mobility impairments. For safe pedestrian use, walkways should have smooth surfaces and be designed to resist heaving. Plant species that will reduce the potential for roots to push up pavement sections should be selected. Ample space must be provided to allow for the future growth of trees and other plantings to ensure they will not encroach upon or damage the walkway.

Walkway edges must be clearly defined and protective. Cobblestone or brick-lined edges provide an aesthetically pleasing, contrasting color and tactile warning for people with visual impairments. Textured concrete or masonry strips can signal upcoming street crossings. A tight corner radius helps calm traffic when needed. The illustration below demonstrates all of these features and the use of bollards, the benefits of which are discussed on the next page.

Curb ramp, walkway, and crosswalk with tactile edges and bollards

There are many other methods of marking edge conditions. Plantings, bollards, spheres, guardrails, or public art can keep motor vehicles from driving onto the sidewalk and at the same time create a detectable edge for pedestrians. They also prevent tripping while walking across curb ramps and reduce jaywalking.

The spheres in the photograph are public artworks constructed from concrete that both mark the sidewalk edge and prevent parking on the sidewalk

Street furniture and plantings prevent walking across a curb cut

The photograph below shows a sidewalk at the same level as an intersection, eliminating the need for curb ramps. Bollards and tactile warnings mark the edge, and the bollards prevent cars from cutting across the corner of the sidewalk.

Bollards marking a curbless corner keep pedestrians safe from careless drivers

Walkways should be constructed from a smooth surface. Bricks or masonry paving products can be used, but only if they have flat surfaces and are even and closely packed enough to create a smooth pedestrian surface. They also should be set into a well-drained and stable subsurface so they are less likely to shift over time. Cobbles should be ground to create a flat walking surface. Tree routes, unstable soil conditions, and frost heaving can all cause uneven sidewalks. Ordinances that require landowners to maintain sidewalks may be necessary to ensure that conditions do not get out of hand and seriously impede safe pedestrian travel.

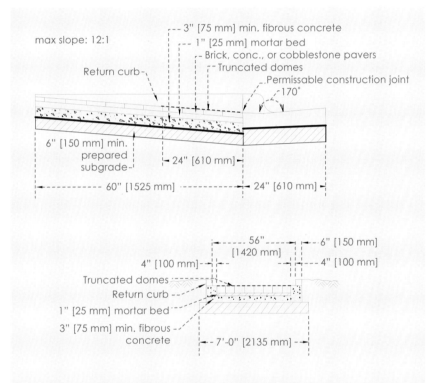

Longitudinal section (top) and cross section (bottom) of curb ramp

In historic districts, historic paving products like cobblestones can be serious problems for older people and people with disabilities when historic preservation authorities insist that walks must be exactly the same as those originally used. Some cities have developed solutions that allow the use of historic pavement materials but also provide accessible accommodations. For example, a single or double track made from concrete or slate can be inset into a cobblestone sidewalk so that wheelchairs, strollers, skates, and other wheeled devices can be used on sidewalks safely and comfortably. Such tracks should be wide enough to accommodate a full range of all the aforementioned devices.

Curb ramps should direct pedestrians in the direction of safe travel and be entirely within the safe crossing area. Crosswalks, like walkways, should have visually distinct and, ideally, tactile edges. Median strips should end before the crosswalk. If this is not possible, the crosswalk should be cut through the island. Bulb corners reduce the length of street crossings and help reduce traffic speed. In addition, they help prevent cars from parking too close to the intersection, allowing motorists to see pedestrians and cross-traffic more easily.

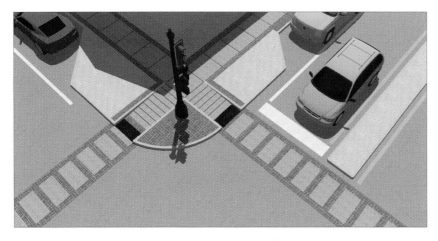

Intersection with median strip, bulb corner, and tactile crosswalk edges

Crossing signals should include pictograms and color-coding so people who do not speak English or who have poor vision can understand. An auditory cue should accompany the "Walk" signal so that those who cannot see or who are not paying attention will know when it is safe to cross. A countdown timer should let pedestrians know how long until the next "walk" signal in addition to the time left until the "don't walk" signal.

Crossing signal with speaker, pictogram, and countdown timer

Block Slopes

There are several ways to provide accessibility to blocks that have sloped topography. This example shows a block where the lots are higher than the street at one end. A second pathway at the higher elevation provides accessibility within the block. A ramp at the end of the block provides access to the upper walkway.

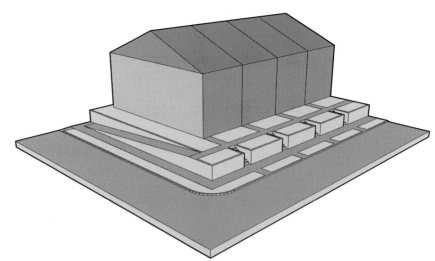

Shared secondary walkway with a ramp at end of the block

Here, the lots are at the same level as the cross street but the road in front of the houses slopes down and away from the cross street. A second pathway is added providing access to the entire block from the cross street. A ramp at the end of the block would provide access to both ends of the block.

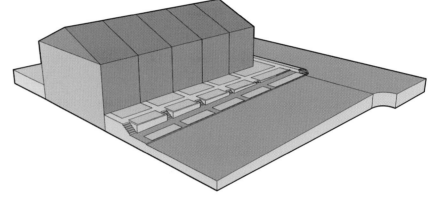

Shared secondary walkway on a sloped site

On a steeply sloped site, a ramp or pathway to the level of one unit is accessible from the adjacent unit's entryway. Access can be ensured with an agreement written into the deeds for the properties.

These strategies all integrate access within the topography, maintain an urban character, and have minimal impact on density. They also support privacy and social contact with the neighbors.

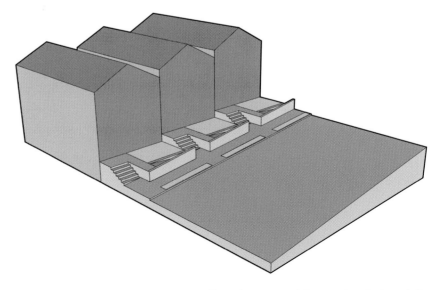

Shared access points on a steeply sloped site

SECTION 5

LOT COMPONENTS

This section of the book identifies the components important for ensuring accessibility within each lot. It explains why each component is important. Examples of lot component assemblies are provided to demonstrate how to evaluate them. Charts and formulas accompany the examples to provide a quick reference for designers.

Overview

Lot components include walkways, driveways, ramps, steps, porches, plantings, and other landscape elements. The house mass as an entirety is treated as a lot component. It is important to remember that even if not described here, anything built on the lot could have a relationship to accessibility. The design of lot components is a key to achieving both Visitable and Lifespan design.

This section begins with pedestrian circulation since it is the dominant mode of circulation on a lot. Accessible means of pedestrian circulation are determined by evaluating grading and the location of walkways. Site and ramp slope must address access concerns and be appropriate for the neighborhood context. Examples illustrating practical applications will be provided throughout this section. In addition to ramp and grading solutions for accessible pedestrian circulation, lifts and vehicle access will be addressed to conclude the section.

⟦t⟧ Helpful tips are indicated by this symbol throughout **Sections 5 and 6**.

⟦t⟧ **Section 7 (Architectural Applications)** identifies many ways to incorporate these strategies without any serious repercussions to aesthetics and other design goals.

Pedestrian Circulation

The most important element of accessible pedestrian circulation is the finished topography of the lot. The lot should be graded such that the slope between vehicle parking and the accessible entry does not exceed 1:20. If this is not possible, a ramp may have to be provided. The formulas provided will help determine the space needed. This is easy to accomplish if thoughtful adjustments are made to the size of the yards, slope, and topography early in the design process. This means thinking about accessibility from the start of land development planning and keeping it in mind at every stage thereafter. This section will illustrate the details of grading, walkway slope requirements, ramp slope requirements, and other concerns of accessible pedestrian circulation.

Key Information:

1:12 = Ramp
1:20 = Sloped walkway
(not a ramp)

x = length of run as measured along the level ground
y = height of destination

$(x \div y) \geq 12$ (ramp)
$(x \div y) \geq 20$ (sloped walkway)

For every 30" [760 mm] in rise of a single ramp, a 60" [1525 mm] landing is required

Ramps greater than 6" [150 mm] in total rise must have railings

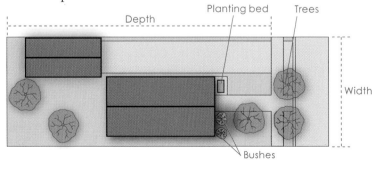

Diagrams using the symbols seen here will be used throughout the section to aid the text and the examples given

Formulas for determining slope

Grading for Pedestrian Circulation

Neighborhood and block topography may limit the options for furnished lot topography. Whatever the existing topography, it is important to remember that site grading is a very useful method to provide access. To ensure access, the following strategies must be used in the design:

▶ One first-floor entry of the house must be at grade;

▶ The lot must be graded up to an entrance level to maintain good drainage;

▶ A ramp or lift must be provided if the grading will not produce an accessible entry.

The slopes to the right are the most basic prototypical lot slopes, although more complex topography is possible.

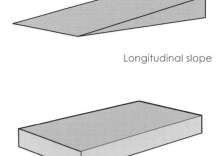

Longitudinal slope

Flat slope

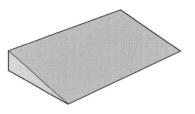

Cross slope

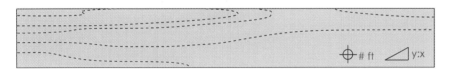

Illustrations in this section use symbols to provide details such as slope and elevation. Contour lines provide more details of topography.

Basic Grading Options

There are several ways in which the site may be graded depending on where the accessible entry is located. The examples below and on the next page depict the most basic options.

The grade can slope between the street and the house to provide an accessible entry on any side of the house.

(t) At a 1:20 slope, if x = 20 ft., then y = 1 ft.
[if x = 6 m, then y = 30 cm]

The grade can slope between the street and the back entry, allowing a front porch to be raised above grade while allowing an approach to the house from either the rear or the front.

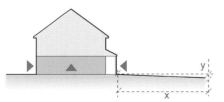

Street to front slope

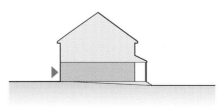

Front to back slope

The grade can slope from an alley to the house to provide an accessible entry at the rear. The example problem below demonstrates a practical application of this grading option.

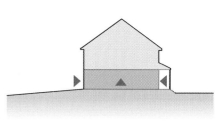

(t) Eliminating steps between the front porch and the interior makes the porch accessible even though the accessible entry may be elsewhere.

Alley to back slope

Problem:

What is the minimum depth of the backyard to avoid the need for a ramp to the rear entry for a rowhouse with a front porch 15 in. [380 mm] above grade?

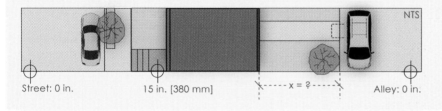

Street: 0 in.   15 in. [380 mm]   x = ?   Alley: 0 in.

NTS

Solution:

Use the formula from page 50 for a sloped walkway (no railing).

$x \div y \geq 20$

$x \geq 20y$

$x \geq 20*15"$ [$x \geq 20*380$ mm]

$x \geq 300"$ or 25' [$x \geq 76$ m]

Therefore, the minimum depth of the rear lot is 300 in. (25 ft.) [76 m] between alley and house.

The grade can slope from a back alley to a front entry to provide a raised front porch or landing at front and rear.

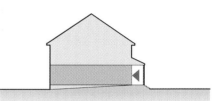

Back to front slope

A combination of front and rear grade slopes can provide no-step access to a side door from both a street and/or alley. See page 55 for an example problem that demonstrates a practical application of this grading option.

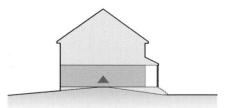

(t) This option provides the flexibility to vary topography at each house without altering the house design.

Front and back slopes

On steep slopes, an accessible entry can provide access to the ground floor. For Visitability, the ground floor level must have accessible livable space and a food preparation area. Plan enough space for a lift for full access to the residence in the future.

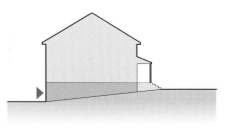

Steep slope

Block Grade Cross Sections

Consider accessibility of lots when planning the block cross section. Studying the cross section carefully helps in understanding how the slope of one lot affects another and the opportunities created by any site.

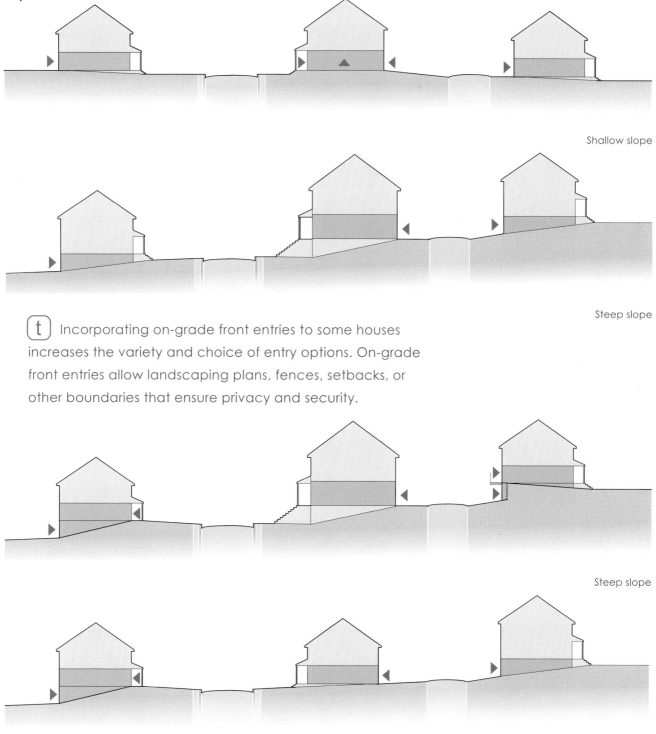

Shallow slope

Steep slope

t Incorporating on-grade front entries to some houses increases the variety and choice of entry options. On-grade front entries allow landscaping plans, fences, setbacks, or other boundaries that ensure privacy and security.

Steep slope

Combination of steep and shallow slopes

Sloped Walkways

A paved walkway is a benefit to all who use a path frequently and a necessity to many people.

Where the block has a slope greater than 1:20 (making direct access from the sidewalk difficult), a second walkway can be added with access at the end of the street. Page 48 in **Section 4 (Block Components)** illustrates more options for access on steep blocks.

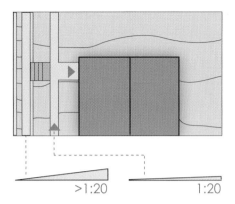

>1:20   1:20

Plan view of accessible second walkway

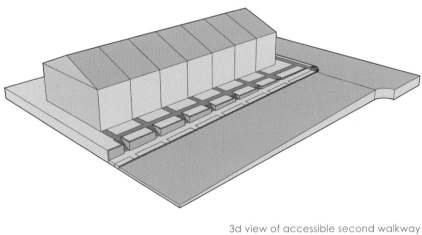

(t) This common walkway crosses all the yards on the block to provide an accessible alternative to stairs without providing ramps or lifts. The retaining wall provides the same privacy and security as a raised porch. This feature also increases social interaction among immediate neighbors. It is very appropriate on busy streets.

3d view of accessible second walkway
See page 48 for this and more accessible block access solutions

A walkway that connects to a side patio makes a good accessible entry. A patio has a variety of uses and provides plenty of space for maneuvering a wheelchair or stroller and parking bicycles.

The side walkway length is related to the elevation of the front porch. The longer the walkway is, the higher the porch can be.

(t) The side walkway can connect to an alley instead of the street.

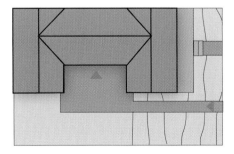

Plan view of side entry walkway and patio

Locating an accessible entry at the side or rear instead of the front often provides the flexibility to include more livability features overall. For example, an accessible side entry may provide more usable space in the front yard and space for wider front steps.

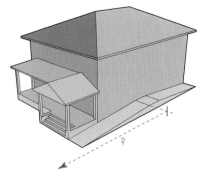

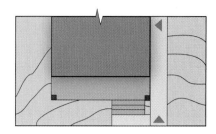

Sloped grade to an accessible side entrance

(t) Side entries can serve two houses at once.

Sloped Walkways Example Problems

Problem 1: (use the table below)
How far back must the accessible entry be from the front of the lot in order to use the sloped driveway condition illustrated above if the side door is 16 in. [405 mm] above street level?

This table is a quick reference to check if a given height and/or length meet accessibility requirements. It is based on the accompanying formulas (first introduced on page 50).

(x ÷ y) ≥ 12 (railings required)   **(x ÷ y) ≥ 20** (no railings required)

Solution:
The door must be at least 26 ft., 8 in. [813 cm] away from the front of the lot for a 1:20 slope.

x = length of ramp (measured along level ground)

y = change in height between destination and ground

Possible Height	ft.	6'8	"	10"1	'	1'2"	1'-4"	1'-6"1	'-8"	1'-10"	2'	2'-2"	2'-4"2	'-6"
	in.	(6")(	8")	(10")	(12")	(14")	(16")	(18")	(20")	(22")	(24")	(26")	(28")	(30")
	mm	[155]	[205]	[255]	[305]	[355]	[405]	[460]	[510]	[560]	[610]	[660]	[715]	[765]
Min. Length Required for Ramp	ft.	6'8	'	10'	12'	14'	16'	18'	20'	22'	24'	26'	28'	30'
	in.	(72")	(96")	(120")	(144")	(168")	(192")	(216")	(240")	(264")	(288")	(312")	(336")	(360")
	cm	[183]	[244]	[305]	[366]	[427]	[488]	[549]	[610]	[671]	[732]	[793]	[854]	[915]
Length Required for Sloped Walkway with No Railings	ft.	10'	13'-4"	16'-8"	20'	23'-4"	26'-8"	30'	33'-4"	36'-8"	40'	43'-4"	46'-8"	50'
	in.	(120")	(160")	(200")	(240")	(280")	(3 20")	(360")	(400")	(440")	(480")	(520")	(560")	(600")
	cm	[305]	[407]	[508]	[610]	[712]	[813]	[914]	[1016]	[1118]	[1220]	[1321]	[1423]	[1524]

P 1   P 2

Problem 2:
A new deck is being built on the side of an existing house that is 40 ft. [480 cm] deep with a floor 26 in. [660 mm] off the ground. Is there enough space for an accessible sloped walkway between the deck and the front of the house?

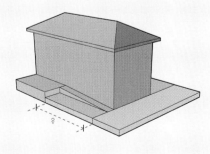

Solution:
Based on the table, there is not enough room for an accessible sloped walkway. At least 26 ft. [793 cm] of space must be left to construct a ramp with railings. Ramps longer than 30 ft. [915 cm], must have a 60 in. [1524 mm] intermediate landing.

Sloped Walkways Example Problem

How long would a walkway from the front porch to the driveway need to be in order to make it accessible and how would the topography need to be changed in order to have an accessible walkway? The site slopes down from NW to SE. The porch is 1 ft. [305 mm] off the ground on the north end. The porch to alley distance is 75 ft. [23 m].

Solution:

Reviewing the contours, we can see that the elevation change between the alley and grade at the porch is 30 in. [760 mm]. The porch height adds another 12 in. [305 mm] making the total elevation change 42 in. [1065 mm]. We know that the distance between the alley and the porch is 75 ft. (900 in.) [23 m]. To see if re-grading would allow an accessible walkway slope, we check the known dimensions with the formulas initially presented on page 50.

$$x \div y \geq 20 \quad \rightarrow \quad 900" \div 42" \geq 20 \quad \rightarrow \quad 21.429 \geq 20 \quad \text{(True)}$$
$$[23\ m \div 1.065\ m \geq 20 \quad \rightarrow \quad 21.596 \geq 20 \quad \text{(True)}]$$

Since the calculation proves true, we know that even after re-grading, an accessible slope for a walkway of 1:20 is possible.

The new contours must be adjusted to provide a consistent slope along the walkway. If the driveway slope is different from the walkway slope, a small retaining wall may be needed. Given a consistent slope under 1:20, the walkway length becomes insignificant as long as it reaches its destination and the driveway slope matches the walkway slope at the point of transfer.

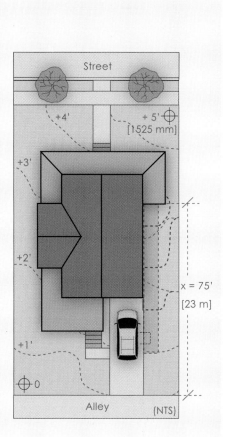

Sloped Landscape Access

A sloped landscape can provide additional accessible routes. The yard could be graded at a 1:20 maximum slope and stabilized using a grass paving system. The result is a raised entry without the appearance of a ramp. It will not meet Visitability regulations, but it can be used to provide access to more than one entrance. This solution may not be appropriate where there is a tendency for ground to settle and heave. Some authorities may not accept this option.*

(t) * See page 60 for more information on "grass paving."

Sloped landscape walkway

Ramp Circulation

A ramp can be fully or partially incorporated into the porch structure. Here, the ramp is completely integrated and shares a landing space with the stairs.

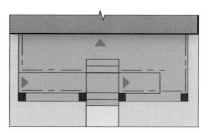

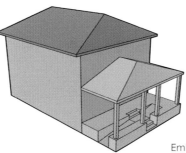

Embedded ramp and stairs with shared landing

 t Framing and foundations can be designed for adding a ramp in the future. This is a useful strategy for a future second accessible entry.

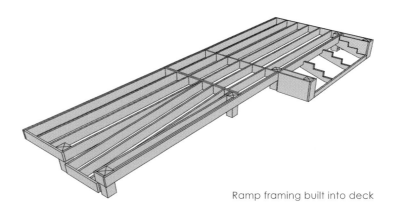

Ramp framing built into deck

The simplest ramp design usually works the best. The landing at the top of the stairs can be used as the landing at the top of the ramp.

t Consult codes for landing dimensions and other requirements.

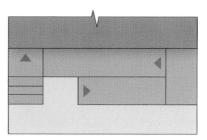

Stairs and ramp with shared landing

A ramp can be a landscape feature. This example combines the upper and lower landing spaces with the stairs. It integrates planting beds with ramp structure, improving the ramp's visual impact.

t The side of the ramp along the sidewalk should be designed to provide a strong territorial boundary. If it is a solid wall, railings will not be visible.

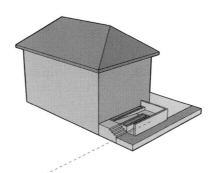

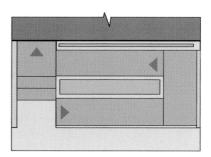

Ramp with planting beds

57

Ramp Circulation Example Problem

Use this chart as a quick reference to determine the dimensions required for a front entry ramp like the one illustrated below. Using the given lot length, you can determine the maximum possible entry height. The chart's dimensions are based on national codes. "Lot width available (W)" refers to the portion of the lot on which structures can be constructed. Planning requirements may make the available lot length and/or width shorter than the actual lot dimensions if a ramp cannot be constructed within required setbacks. Be sure to consider this when choosing the "lot width available (W)."

Lot Width Available (W)	16' (192") [488 cm]	20' (240") [610 cm]	24' (288") [732 cm]	28' (336") [853 cm]	32' (384") [975 cm]	36' (432") [1.1 m]	40'+ (480")+ [1.22 m]
For 2 Even Ramp Sections							
x max	6' (72') [183 cm]	10' (120") [305 cm]	14' (168") [427 cm]	18' (216") [549 cm]	22' (264") [671 cm]	26' (312") [792 cm]	30' (360") [914 cm]
y max	6" (6") [150 mm]	10" (10") [255 mm]	1'-2" (14") [355 mm]	1'-6" (18") [460 mm]	1'-10" (22") [560 mm]	2'-2" (26") [660 mm]	2'-6" (30") [765 mm]
h max	1' (12") [305 mm]	1'-8" (20") [510 mm]	2'-4" (28") [715 mm]	3' (36") [915 mm]	3'-8" (44") [1120 mm]	4'-4" (52") [1320 mm]	5' (60") [1525 mm]
If Stairs Are Between Ramp Sections							
z min	2' (24") [610 mm]	2'-8" (32") [815 mm]	3'-4" (40") [1015 mm]	4'-2" (50") [1270 mm]	5' (60") [1525 mm]	5'-10" (70") [178 cm]	6'-8" (80") [203 cm]
f	8' (96") [244 cm]	8'-8" (104") [264 cm]	9'-4" (112") [284 cm]	10'-2" (122") [310 cm]	11' (132") [335 cm]	11'-10" (142") [361 cm]	12'-8" (152") [386 cm]

5 ft [1525 mm]

5 ft [1525 mm]

Problem:

Can a switchback ramp fit in front of the house? The available lot width is 22 ft. [671 cm]. The available lot depth is 11 ft. [335 cm].

Solution:

Interpolating from the above chart using W=22 ft. [671 cm], we find that the maximum height of one ramp section (y) is 12 in. [305 mm]; thus the porch can be no higher (h) than 24 in. [610 mm]. To fit the stairs where shown, the planting box (z) must be at least 36 in. [910 mm], meaning that the front yard (f) must be at least 9 ft. [274 cm]. Since the landing dimension must be at least 60 in. by 60 in. [1525 mm], and the door is flush with the house, another 24 in. [610 mm] must be added making the total yard width needed 11 ft. [335 cm]. The ramp will fit within the lot, as long as the porch is no higher than 24 in. [610 mm].

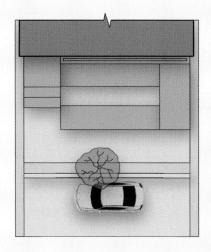

Plan diagram

Lifts

Although they take up less space than a ramp, lifts are not desirable solutions but they may be necessary where flood plain restrictions make other solutions infeasible. They are generally less aesthetically pleasing and are more costly than other solutions. They also are prone to mechanical failure and need battery backup for power failures. The operator must know how to use the lift. Lifts are most commonly available with a gate on two opposite sides (straight-through circulation plan), but 90-degree turn lifts are also available. Lifts are not generally acceptable as a means to meet accessibility requirements in housing.

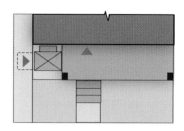

(t) Use a straight-through lift layout because 90-degree lifts are larger and more difficult to use.

Lift next to porch

As with ramps, porch cutouts can be prepared in advance and lifts installed when needed. Pre-installing the necessary pad and foundation is also helpful. Remember to plan space for the lift platform, gate swing, and the mechanical housing.

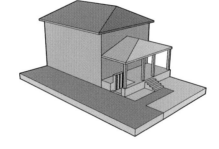

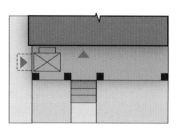

Lift built into porch

Vehicle Accommodations

This section has focused primarily on pedestrian circulation within the lot thus far, but accommodating motor vehicles is also a major component of lot planning of housing with off-street parking. Driveways can also serve as an accessible path of travel. This and the next page describe how to accommodate vehicles on the site so that people with mobility impairments can use them.

Driveways can be sloped gradually to reduce or eliminate the need for ramps. Visitability requirements allow the accessible path of travel to the house to begin at the end of a driveway. The Fair Housing Act allows this approach in multifamily housing under some conditions. By careful planning of the unloading area, accessibility can be provided without an extremely wide driveway. The unloading area should be at least 36 inches [915 mm] wide and 48 inches [1220 mm] long plus an additional 48 inches [1220 mm] beyond the end of the lift.

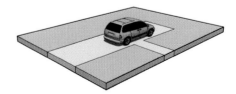

Accessible driveway with walkway

An accessible route from the garage to the house is needed. In cold regions, direct access from a garage to a house is desirable for all residents. The floor of a garage can slope down slightly to the garage door. New residential codes do not require a level change between garage and house (See International Residential Code).

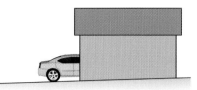

Garage with sloped floor

(t) In Visitable housing, the driveway can slope at 1:12 without railings under certain conditions. See Appendix A: Ramps (1006.5.4).

Access to public walkways is needed where parking is on the street, alley, or off site. Curb ramps provide accessible street parking if they connect to the sidewalk at on-street parking spaces. To ensure that no one else will park in them, such spaces should be marked using a painted curb or pavement line markings and signs.

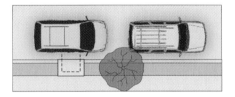

Accessible street parking space

Alternative Paving Solutions

Balancing paved space with green space can be difficult, particularly where lots are small. Architects and planners have a responsibility to preserve green space, which is important for both aesthetic and environmental reasons. Many homeowners have multiple vehicles, boats, and RVs. It is a misconception that the only way to accommodate these vehicles is more paved driveway. An alternative to concrete or asphalt is a grass paving system that allows grass to grow through a grid of reinforced concrete or plastic. The result is a stable, drivable surface with the appearance of a regular lawn. It is strong enough to support large vehicles and it can connect to an acceptable paved accessible route to an entry. Grass paving can address the needs of a diverse group of homeowners while maintaining a pleasing appearance.

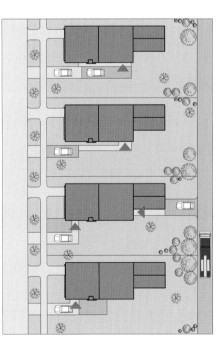

Possible grass paving locations

(t) Use grass paving for alleys in warm-weather climates. This gives access to emergency vehicles and other services without the need for a wide asphalt or concrete road. Grass paving can also be used at the ends of lots bordering on alleys to provide overflow parking.

SECTION 6

HOUSE COMPONENTS

This section describes the components that support inclusive design within a home. Basic strategies of Visitable design are described. Additional recommendations are provided to demonstrate Lifespan design. Examples are provided to illustrate applications of these strategies.

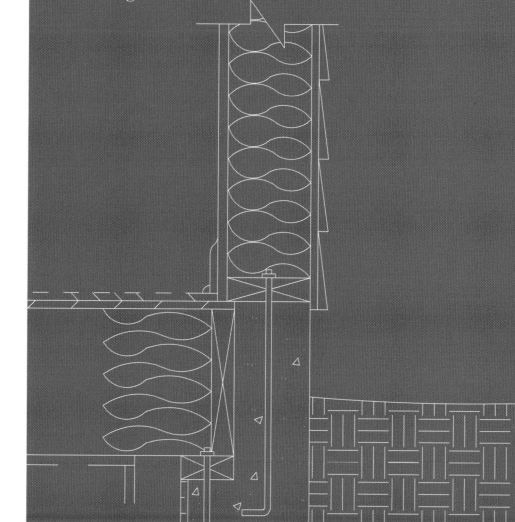

Overview

While recommendations are provided for other features, this section focuses on the most critical issues for space planning: design for wheeled mobility. Designing access for this group provides generous space clearances for all users and makes a house feel more spacious and comfortable. This provides a foundation for future upgrades toward Lifespan design. Critical components include doorways, vertical and horizontal circulation, bathrooms, and kitchens. These are the permanent and relatively inflexible parts of a house. It is important to note that careful placement of furniture and fixtures and following basic strategies for providing accessibility for design decisions not discussed here also contribute to the success of the final product.

(t) Dimensions are given in imperial units with their metric equivalents in the accompanying brackets.

Basic Space Clearances

As a rule of thumb, a clear floor area of 30" x 48" [760 mm x 1220 mm] will accommodate most manual wheelchairs with average-sized occupants (figure 6-1). These are minimum code dimensions. Adding more space will accommodate larger people and power chairs as well. Scooters require even more space. Scooters are not intended for in-home use, although many people are using them inside homes. A clear floor area is required in and around all appliances, furniture, and fixtures to allow wheelchair users to access and use them safely. At a minimum, a parallel or perpendicular approach to the fixtures should be designed into the plan. Rooms need to be designed to provide space for maneuvering outside the space taken up by door swings.

A more generous room design allows a person in a wheelchair to turn around inside it. Fixtures and/or architectural elements need to be 60 inches [1525 mm] apart to provide for a minimum turning area (figure 6-2) for average-sized individuals using manual chairs. More space is needed for clear floor areas to accommodate larger people, power chairs, and scooters. Therefore, provide a few more inches where possible. They will make a big difference in convenience for everyone.

Visitable

indicates an example of Visitable accommodations

Lifespan

indicates an example of Lifespan accommodations

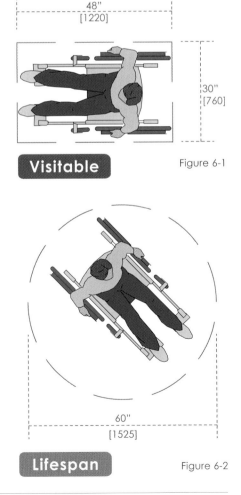

48"
[1220]

30"
[760]

Visitable

Figure 6-1

60"
[1525]

Lifespan

Figure 6-2

Basic Reach Ranges

Visitable **Lifespan**

The placement of switches, wall outlets, shelves, and other items is an important consideration.

Visitability requirements specify 15 to 48 inches [390 mm to 1220 mm] off the ground for items to be reachable to a person using a wheelchair.

A Lifespan house benefits from a narrower range as illustrated at the far right. This makes reaching easier for someone who cannot easily bend over and makes many tasks more convenient to accomplish for all, especially those that require lifting.

Doorways

Narrow doorways are the most common interior barrier to people who use wheelchairs. However, for long-term use, the clearance in front of doorways is almost as important. Depending on the approach to the door and in which direction the door swings, a wheelchair user may need more space to turn toward the door at a good approach angle, reach the handle, and stay clear of the door swing. Visitability standards do not require maneuvering clearances at doors, but they are easy to provide given careful space planning.

(t) Doorways must have at least a 32 inch [815 mm] wide clear opening. To accommodate larger people and chairs, consider a 34 inch [865 mm] opening.

Visitable

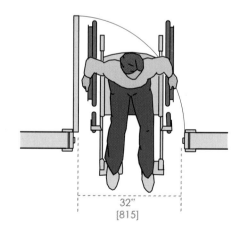

It can often be beneficial to all homes to have wider doorways. For example, they enhance the occupant's ability to move furniture and appliances that would otherwise be difficult or even impossible with narrow doorways. For this reason, most front doors are already 36 inches wide (34 inches clear opening) [915 mm / 865 mm].

Door Approach   Lifespan

Although not required for Visitability, these guidelines for maneuvering clearances at doors should be implemented whenever possible. A Lifespan house should incorporate all of these approach guidelines at every door.

Pull Side, Latch Side: Parallel to Wall

A pull side, latch side approach requires some space for maneuvering as the door swings. As a person using a wheelchair approaches, he or she must get in front of the door to reach the handle, and then move out of the way of the door swing before proceeding through the doorway.

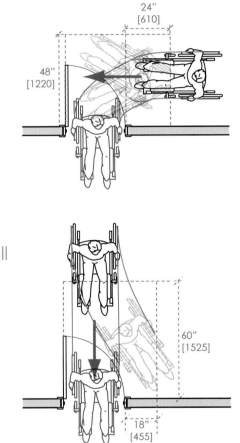

Pull Side, Front: Perpendicular to Wall

While the pull side, latch side of the door should have at least an 18 inch [455 mm] clear space, ideally it should be 24 inches [610 mm]. The latch clearance provides room for a person in a wheelchair to move into a position where he or she can grab the handle.

Pull Side, Hinge Side: Parallel to Wall

The most difficult approach to a door is the pull side, hinge side maneuver. Avoid this approach wherever possible because of its difficulty and the large space required. As a rule, the greater the width, the less latch-side clearance is needed. For example, if there is a 60 inch [1525 mm] clearance width, then only a 36 inch [915 mm] latch clearance is needed. If there is only a 54 inch [1370 mm] width, a 42 inch [1065 mm] latch clearance is needed.

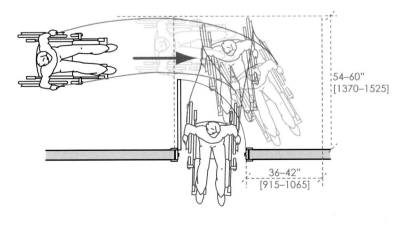

Push Side, Hinge & Latch Sides: Parallel to Wall

A push side approach is easier than a pull side approach because the wheelchair user does not have to maneuver around the swing of the door. However, he or she does need to move far enough forward to reach the handle and push the door open. Pushing the door open is much easier from a more forward position because the operator has better mechanical advantage. Clearly, people who can walk benefit from these clearances as well as wheelchair users. Moreover, the extra space can always be utilized if residents desire by using them for decorative objects or small furniture. Careful space planning can therefore facilitate use of doors by everyone.

(t) Plan bedroom doorways to open into widened hallway areas. This makes the house feel more spacious and provides opportunities for decoration and conversation.

Push Side, Front: Perpendicular to Wall

A 12 inch [305 mm] latch clearance gives a wheelchair user enough space to get close to the door when operating the latch in this direction.

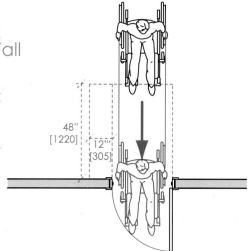

Door Hardware   Lifespan

People using canes, crutches, walkers, or wheelchairs, and those with visual impairments all can have difficulty using doors. Walking aids sometimes get in the way of pulling a door shut. Children and people with visual impairments can be injured when approaching a door from the pull side if there is no view panel to see people approaching on the other side. Doors with mechanical closers can be very difficult for someone in a wheelchair and those with limited strength to use. Some people will need automated doors where codes require self-closing devices (e.g. entry doors to apartments). Thus, providing electrical supply nearby for future installation of automated doors is a good idea.

A lever handle allows a person to open a door with little effort. This is beneficial to people who have difficulty using their hands or whose hands are full. An extra handle can be added to the push side of doors to allow a person using a wheelchair to close the door behind them with less effort. A solid area at the bottom of a door facilitates wheelchair use because people can use their feet and the footrests to push doors open.

(t) Install a cabinet pull (see figure) on the push side of doors when making adaptations for wheelchair users.

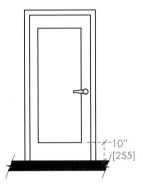

Door with window

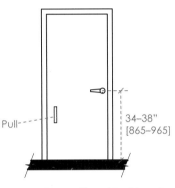

Pull

34–38"
[865–965]

Door with cabinet handle

Thresholds & Surface Changes   Visitable

Thresholds and surface changes must be very small if they have abrupt edges. This benefits people with limited gait as well as wheelchair users.

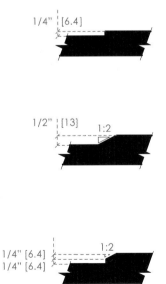

1/4" [6.4]

1/2" [13]   1:2

1/4" [6.4]   1:2
1/4" [6.4]

No-step entries with low thresholds

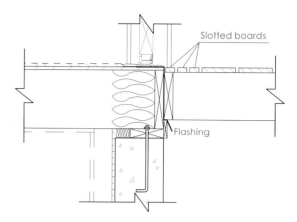

Low-threshold door to porch or deck

An exterior door with a low threshold should have a roof overhang and have good drainage outside to prevent water infiltration. Overhangs are especially needed in cold climates when the door opens out to prevent blockage by snow. In the figure on the right, boards with drainage spaces between them replace the typical decking near the threshold, allowing water and melting snow to drain away from the threshold area.

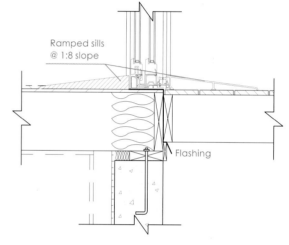

Construction detail of sliding door with ramped sill

Sliding doors have especially high thresholds, but if the deck or porch is constructed to be flush with the inside floor, a ramped sill can be placed on both sides and be designed to match the surrounding decor.

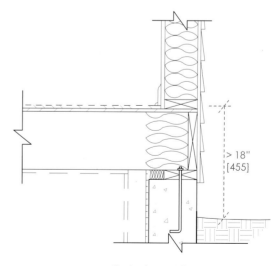

Typical wood-frame construction

Conventional wood-frame construction (illustrated on the right) typically has steps at entries because floor joists usually lie on top of the foundation wall which protrudes above the ground to keep the wood away from water and insects. This typically results in the finished floor of a conventional wood-frame home being at least 18 inches [455 mm] above grade.

A wood-frame home built as described on the previous page would require at least an 18 foot [548 cm] ramp to connect the ground to the first-floor level. One way to eliminate the need for a ramp is to offset the inside of the foundation to provide a ledge for resting joists. The outside part of the offset area protects the floor framing from water. A reverse brick ledge (illustrated on the right) can be used to do this. This yields only a 6 inch [155 mm] difference in height, which is the recommended distance between grade and wood materials. A slight slope to achieve a no-step entry is easy at this height.

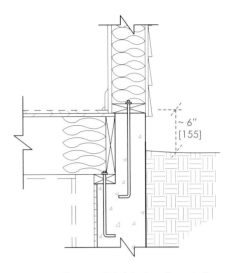

Reverse brick-ledge foundation section at wall

Gravel fill can be added around the perimeter of the foundation to create positive drainage near the door and wooden materials. A metal grate or concrete paver can be used to span the gravel strip as in the illustration on the right and the photo on page 66.

(t) See Appendix B for additional section detail options.

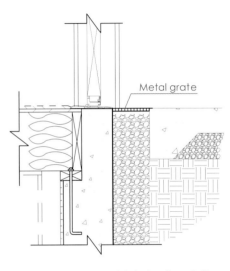

Reverse brick-ledge foundation section at entry

Vertical Circulation

A one-story home is the most obvious way to ensure that an entire home is accessible for everyone. Many factors such as cost, lot size, and surrounding context often make a one-story plan undesirable. The next best option is a two-story home with all of the essential features on the accessible floor. This includes a living space, food preparation area, full bathroom or at least a half bathroom (ideally with the ability to be expanded or converted into a full bathroom), a room that is large enough to be transformed into a bedroom with a closet and some privacy, and a laundry room. The minimum requirements of Visitability can be accomplished without access to the main living floor of a home if one living space and another food preparation area – for example, a family room with a small kitchenette – are provided at the accessible level. However, this minimal approach is not desirable if the main living floor can be made fully accessible.

A space for a future residential elevator can be included to extend access to the entire house – a Lifespan design feature. This can be accomplished by stacking two larger closets and framing out a hole in the ceiling/floor. If the laundry is in the basement, plan the shaft location to reach there as well. The shaft space should be large enough to accommodate an elevator designed for use with a wheelchair. Building codes may have specific requirements for such shafts, particularly in buildings with more than one unit in them.

Staircase Guidelines

These guidelines for staircase design provide the greatest amount of safety and comfort:

▶ Interior staircases should have a 7-inch tall riser and an 11-inch deep tread [175, 280 mm]. Exterior staircases should have 4 to 7 inch [100–175 mm] risers and 11 to 14 inch [280–355 mm] treads, not including the nosing. Any riser height or tread width within these ranges will provide safe and comfortable proportions. The riser-tread formulas found in guidebooks on staircase design are not substantiated by research, and their use can lead to sizes outside these ranges.

▶ The width of the staircase should be between 36 and 44 inches [915–1120 mm].

▶ The curve on the nosing should have a maximum radius of ½ inch [12 mm] and should not protrude more than 1½ inches [38 mm]. Risers can be sloped or the nosing can be partially sloped (as shown in the figure on the right) with a minimum of a 60-degree angle from the horizontal.

▶ The riser, tread, and nosing dimensions should remain consistent through the entire staircase.

▶ Landings need to be at least as wide and as long as the stair width. A run of stairs should not exceed 12 feet [366 cm] in height without a landing.

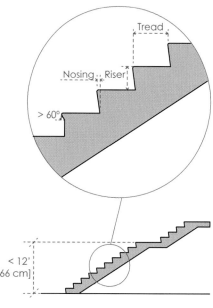

Staircase section

Staircase plan

Staircase Types

The type of staircase has an impact on safety and comfort of use. It is important to consider the advantages and disadvantages of each.

Straight-run staircases are the most common and easiest to fit into a plan. A disadvantage is that a person falling on them falls a greater distance from the top than on other staircase configurations.

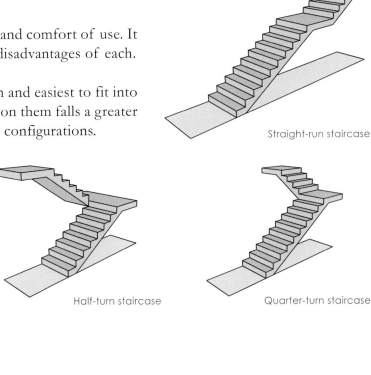

Straight-run staircase

Half-turn and **quarter-turn** staircases take up more space in plan but, depending on the house layout, a turn may be an advantage. They also reduce the distance of falls.

Half-turn staircase

Quarter-turn staircase

Winding staircases are any type of staircase with treads that are narrower at one end than the other such as pie-shaped treads. **Circular** staircases are special winding staircases in which all treads are uniform. Using winding staircases can be difficult. Since the tread depth varies along its width, one foot has to be placed differently than the other, making the user's gait awkward. If the plan of the staircase is not regular, e.g. a circular or a consistent arc, the tread depth will vary even more from step to step. Winding staircases are not desirable, but they can save space in plan and therefore are often used in affordable housing. They should be kept to a minimum where they are not regular, and preferably only used where a staircase changes direction. The smallest depth on any winder should be at least 10 inches [255 mm]. If winding staircases have high guardrails or walls along both edges, injury from a fall could be minimized since the fall will have a greater probability of being interrupted.

NOT RECOMMENDED

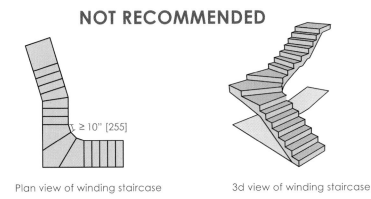

Plan view of winding staircase

3d view of winding staircase

NOT RECOMMENDED

Plan view of circular staircase

3d view of circular staircase

Spiral staircases are very tight winding staircases where one side of the treads is no more than a few inches in depth. These, and **ship's ladders**, occupy a minimum amount of floor space. Building codes permit their use only as private staircases in individual dwelling units. They may be dangerous, especially for children and the elderly. For safety reasons, they should be avoided whenever possible as the only means of circulation to reach essential features of a home. They should only be used in places where they would receive infrequent use such as an attic or loft storage space.

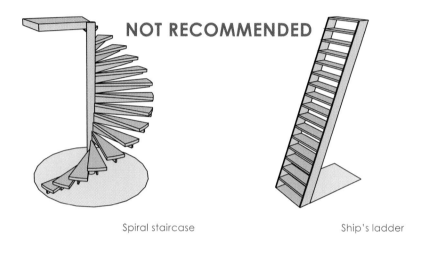

NOT RECOMMENDED

Spiral staircase   Ship's ladder

Handrails & Guardrails

Handrails should be smooth and easy to grasp. The diagrams below depict dimensions that provide a secure grip. Handrails for stairs should be continuous with smooth joints. The height should be 36 inches [915 mm] above the stair treads. At the bottom of the staircase, the railing should end at the ground or lower landing, not at the last tread. At the top, the handrail should extend beyond the last riser by at least at least 12 inches [305 mm], as shown in the diagram on the next page.

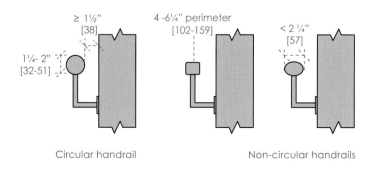

≥ 1½" [38]   4 -6¼" perimeter [102-159]   < 2 ¼" [57]

1¼- 2" [32-51]

Circular handrail   Non-circular handrails

Guardrails are required to protect the open or glazed sides of stairs and ramps. To prevent a small child from falling through a guardrail, a 4 inch [100 mm] sphere must not be able to pass through any opening in the guardrail. Guardrails are also needed to protect open or glazed sides of porches, and unenclosed floor and roof openings.

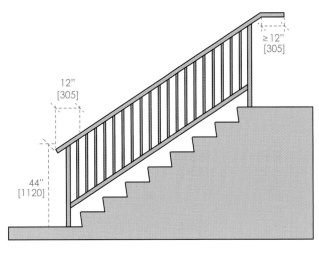

Guardrails

Ramps

Generally, ramps cannot be used to traverse level changes greater than about 6 inches [150 mm] inside a home because of the space required for higher ramps. If they are to be used, they should meet the requirements described in **Section 5**, including a 36-inch [915 mm] minimum clear width between curbs or handrails. Curbs should be at least 2 inches high on each side of the ramp to prevent slipping off the ramp. Other methods can be used to prevent slips off the ramp surface, for example, closely spaced vertical rails. Ramps should have a maximum slope of 1:12. A lower slope is preferable where there is enough space to have a longer run. On each end of a ramp run, there should be a clear space of at least 60 inches in length. Ramps with a rise less than or equal to 6 inches [150 mm] or a horizontal run less than or equal to 30 inches [760 mm] do not need handrails. All other ramps should have handrails along both sides. Handrails should be 36 inches above the ramp surface and should extend at least 12 inches horizontally beyond the sloped part of the ramp. Consult accessibility codes for more requirements on ramp length and proper landing dimensions if ramps are planned.

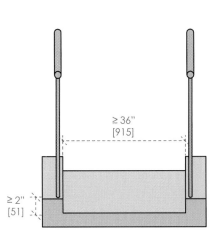

Ramp section

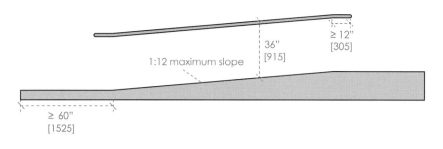

36"
[915]

≥ 12"
[305]

1:12 maximum slope

≥ 60"
[1525]

(t) Refer to **Section 5** for charts and example problems dealing with ramps.

Common Practices & Ways to Improve

The front steps' railings on the left are metal and wood that look inexpensive and awkward compared to the all-wood railings in the picture on the right.

The long continuous staircase on the left does not look very pleasing, and the lack of a landing increases the risk of a serious injury during a fall. The staircase on the right is shorter, reducing the risk of serious injury. By fitting the house into the topography carefully, not only could the staircase be shorter, but a sloped driveway to an on-grade back entry is possible.

Hallways & Passages

Circulation spaces should be at least 36 inches [915 mm] wide. An intersecting 36 inch [915 mm] passage will provide a minimal space to allow one person to get out of the way of a second. Each arm of the intersection should be at least 60 inches [1525 mm] before there is another change of direction to provide enough space for wheelchair users. Note that these are minimal dimensions. For more convenient use, at least one link at an intersection should be 42 inches [1065 mm].

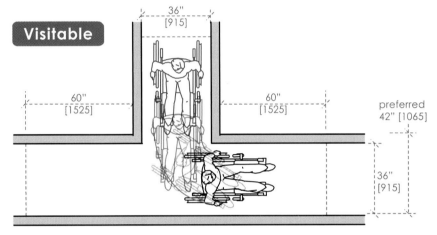

Widening the hallway to 42 inches [1065 mm] will provide more convenience and allow an ambulatory person to squeeze past a person in a wheelchair. Sixty inches allows two wheelchairs to pass. If a hallway is narrower than 60 inches [1525 mm], any dead ends must have a space 60 inches by 60 inches [1525 mm by 1525 mm] to allow a person in a wheelchair to turn around, or some other accommodation that allows reversal of direction. Adding an additional 18 inches [455 mm] in length as shown provides extra space and comfort when turning around. Note that space for two people in wheelchairs to pass is not necessary in a typical home, but a 60 inch by 60 inch widened area [1525 mm by 1525 mm] near doorways is very advantageous for convenient circulation by all residents.

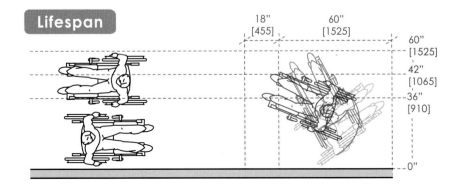

Bathroom Fixtures

Lavatory Approach

Although a parallel approach to a lavatory can be used in Visitable and Fair Housing dwelling units, it is not easy to use for a wheelchair user because it requires twisting one's body. The perpendicular approach is preferred because the user's body aligns with the fixture. Knee clearance under the fixture is required to make it usable in this position. A Lifespan design allows both approaches.

Bathtub Parallel Approach

The bathtub should have a minimum clear space of 30 inches by 60 inches [760 mm by 1525 mm] along the side. A lavatory may be located within the clear floor area if knee clearance is provided underneath. A more accessible design will have a 30 inch [760 mm] deep clear space adjacent to the entire length of the bathtub. This would allow a person to enter the tub near the front or back wall from either a forward or a backward approach, and to more easily reach the tub and shower controls.

Bathtub Perpendicular Approach

This approach requires that the user be able to stand and pivot his or her body while entering the tub. The toilet also blocks convenient access to the tub faucets. A lavatory with knee clearance is preferable next to a tub to allow a parallel approach.

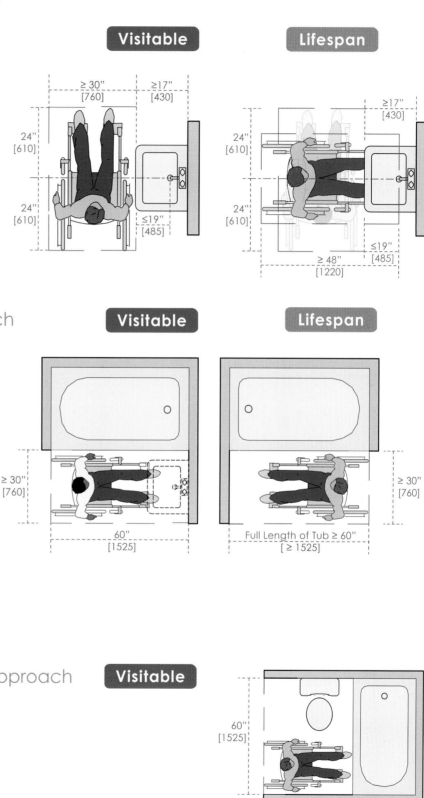

Walk-in Bathtub   `Lifespan`

The walk-in bathtub is advantageous for anyone who has difficulty climbing or transferring over a tub rim. Such tubs are the same length as a standard-size tub but they are wider. The tub depth allows the occupant to maintain a seated position while also being submerged.

The tub door reduces the risk of falling while climbing over the rim and is convenient for caregivers, but there is a step and the door is narrow.

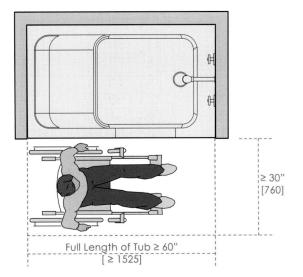

When using a walk-in bathtub in a design, it is important to include a heat lamp over the tub due to the length of time a person must remain in the tub while it fills and drains. Tubs with a quick-fill and drain feature are preferred.

Transfer Shower   `Visitable`

This type of shower might be found in a Visitable bathroom. At least 30 inches [760 mm] of clear floor in front of the shower is necessary, but 36 inches [915 mm] is preferable. It is also desirable to have the clearance extend at least 12 inches [150 mm] beyond the rear wall of the shower. These showers are not recommended for dwellings designed specifically for people with mobility impairments. Bathing in a seated position in a minimally sized shower can be difficult for anyone. It is also difficult to assist another person in a small shower stall like this. The accessible shower is about 6 inches [125 mm] wider and deeper than minimal shower stalls. The added space makes a significant difference in comfort for all users.

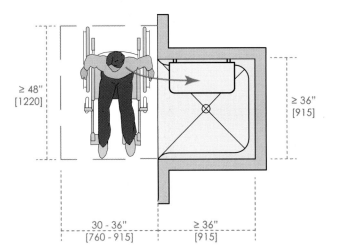

Roll-in Shower

This type of shower is easier and more comfortable to use by everyone. A shower wheelchair is specially designed to be wheeled directly into the shower. It is easier to give assistance and help children in a shower of this size. These chairs also reduce the risk of falling.

(t) There should never be a curb at a roll-in shower. Instead, a low threshold like the one described below, in combination with a properly sized drain and a sufficient slope inside the shower, is enough to keep water inside the shower.

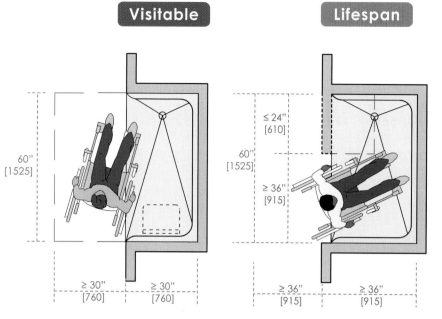

This cross section detail shows how the floor would need to be constructed for a no-step shower entry. Joists under the shower would need to be smaller to avoid the need for a curb.

a Stud wall
b Shower rod @ 76" [1930] A.F.F.
c Adjustable showerhead
d 24" [610] Grab bar @ 36" [915] A.F.F.
e 36" [915] Grab bar @ 36" [915] A.F.F.
f Top of membrane behind wall
g Tile floor @1:50 slope
h Tile setting bed
j Two-stage floor drain with weep holes
k Blocking

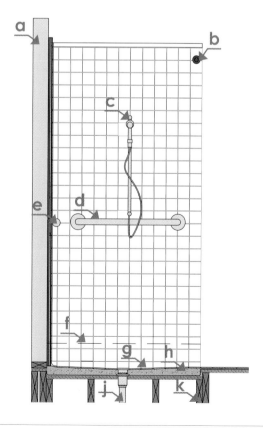

Toilets:

Parallel Approach

This approach occupies the least amount of space. However, it requires a wheelchair user to travel a greater distance when transferring to the toilet.

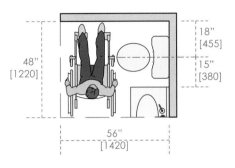

Forward Approach Visitable

This approach allows wheelchair users to approach the toilet feet-first either straight ahead or at an angle.

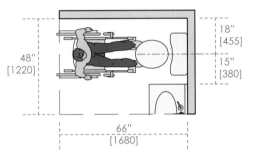

Parallel or Forward Approach Lifespan

This is the preferred transfer approach because it allows a parallel transfer reducing the transfer distance to a minimum and also allows other approaches.

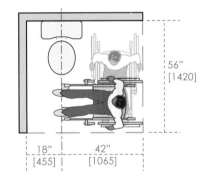

Universal Clearances

These clearances allow all types of transfers and accommodate larger wheelchairs.

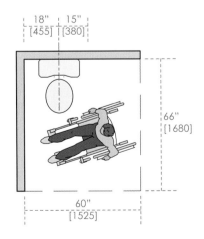

Bathroom Layout

Half Bath **Visitable**

This is the minimal space for an accessible bathroom. Note that the length of the toilet is a critical dimension in this plan. It has to be called out in the drawings or the toilet should be carefully specified by model. In addition, the door must open outward.

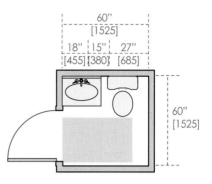

Full Bath with Single Door on Long Side **Visitable**

Although locating the door on the long side of a rectangular room provides good potential for wheeled mobility access, note that many of these examples are not ideal because the toilets are not located next to a wall where a long grab bar can be installed.

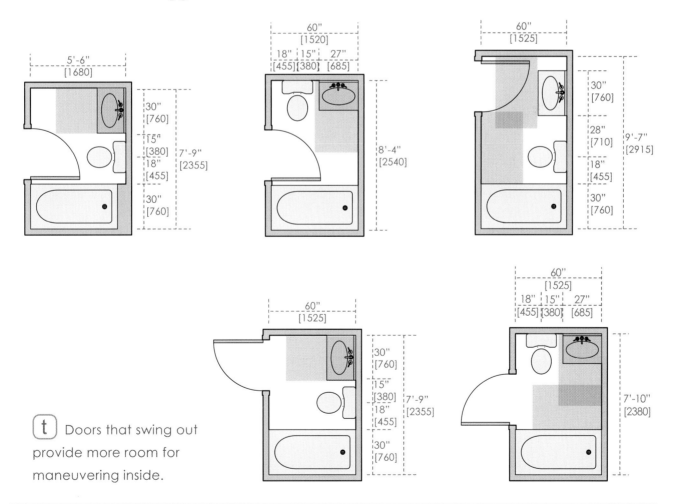

(t) Doors that swing out provide more room for maneuvering inside.

Single Door on Short Side   Visitable

While providing limited accessibility, this door location makes it nearly impossible to locate a long grab bar next to the toilet. The length of the toilet can also impede access through the door.

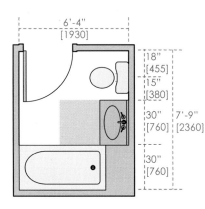
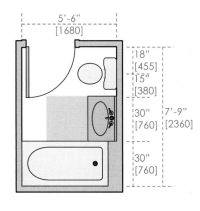
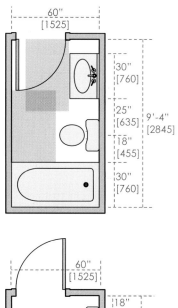

(t) Doors that swing out can reduce the bathroom width in addition to providing more maneuvering room.

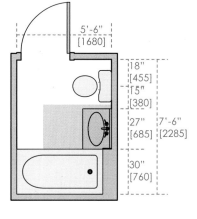
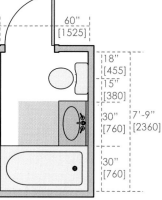

Two Doors on Adjacent Sides   Visitable

When a second door is added, the bathroom should be designed so that wheelchair clearance is unobstructed with both doors open.

(t) If the toilet and door are both in the center, more depth is needed to ensure that the door can be closed when it opens inward.

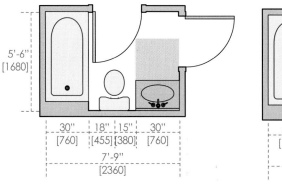
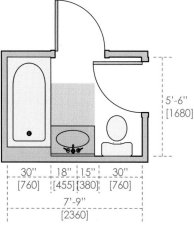

Lifespan Bathrooms Lifespan

In these examples, the depth of the bathroom has been increased compared to the Visitable version, providing more convenience and, in particular, better access to the tub. All of these bathrooms have enough wall length to add a long grab bar next to the toilet. Note how the larger bathrooms are very generous and luxurious as well as fully accessible and amenable to assisted bathing.

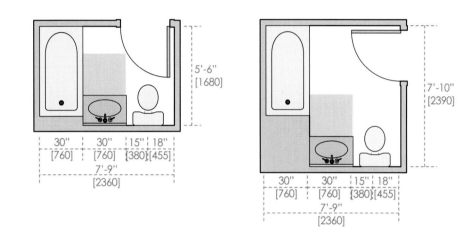

Examples of lifespan designed bathrooms

Lifespan Bathrooms   **Lifespan**

Swinging the door out allows the bathroom to be much more efficient while still fully adaptable for Lifespan needs. Note that they do not require any more floor space than many less accessible plans. Most wheelchair users could turn around in these bathrooms. Offsetting the lavatory with the tub or shower provides ideal access to the shower controls from outside.

(t) The additional space in Lifespan bathrooms can be filled with removable storage units but not fixed cabinetry.

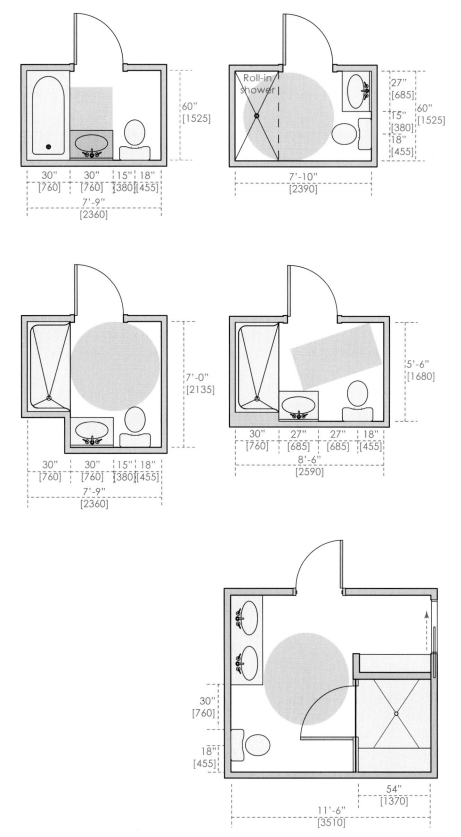

Kitchen Work Stations & Cabinetry   Lifespan

Varied workstation heights in a kitchen are an essential feature of Lifespan design because they increase convenience and reduce effort for all.

Countertops at sinks should be set at 36 inches [915 mm] high. A counter that is 42 inches [1065 mm] above the floor is at a good height for writing and reading while standing, but not necessarily good for heavy work. Depending on the task, 35 to 42 inch [890-1065 mm] heights may be needed for a person who is standing. A person who is seated needs a work station as close to knee height as possible. A 28 to 32 inch [710–810 mm] counter height satisfies this requirement for many. Ideally, several height options between 42 and 28 inches [1065, 710 mm] would be available. In the image on the top, there are three different counter heights; two counters including one with a sink at 36 inches [915 mm], a sitting area and sink at 28 inches [710 mm], and a raised area above the dishwasher at 42 inches [1065 mm]. Adaptable height work stations provide additional benefits. Concepts for designing adaptable cabinets can be found on page 85.

Varied height work stations w/ knee space

A raised oven can allow an oven door to be at the same height as an adjacent counter. This facilitates the transfer of hot and/or heavy items. This makes a wall-mounted oven easier for everyone to use. It also facilitates cleaning, although self-cleaning ovens greatly reduce the frequency of human maintenance required. A side-by-side refrigerator allows easy access to both the refrigerator and freezer. Built-in ice and cold-water dispensers are a convenient feature for all.

Wall-mounted oven

Raising a dishwasher 6 to 10 inches [155–255 mm] off the floor, as shown in the image on the bottom, reduces the effort required to load or empty its contents to a nearby counter. It also provides an opportunity to have a workstation with a high countertop as discussed above.

Access to storage spaces in the kitchen is another important consideration of Lifespan design. Appropriately designed kitchen storage spaces benefit all. The examples on the next page facilitate maintenance and organization of goods and utensils while allowing easy access for people with different abilities.

Raised dishwasher

There are many simple ways to improve the accessibility of storage cabinets in kitchens. The images on the right provide some examples. Lazy Susan shelves, sliding drawers in base cabinets, and the addition of extra drawers are useful for everyone. The image on the bottom shows a cabinet door with storage shelves attached to the door so that when it is opened, equipment and supplies are easily accessible without reaching into the cabinet itself. The first shelf of wall-mounted cabinets over counters should not be higher than 48 inches from the floor. Full-size storage units can provide fully accessible storage space.

Lazy Susan

Another option for ensuring Lifespan access is the use of adaptable cabinetry. Adaptable cabinetry allows a kitchen to be adjusted over time to meet occupant needs and preferences. Since people with different kinds or levels of disability have different needs over time, the kitchen should be adaptable even if the home is designed specifically for someone with a disability. Removable cabinet fronts and bases under the sink and work stations can provide a knee clearance. Fronts of cabinets can appear conventional and detach to provide accessibility. The backsplash needs to be larger than normal to accommodate the lower counter positions. Moreover, the base cabinet at either end of the adjustable counter and adjacent appliances must have finished sides.

Sliding drawers in cabinet

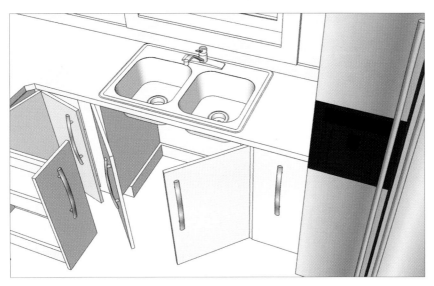

Kitchen with lazy Susan, pullout storage shelves, and removable base under sink

Pullout storage shelves

The next page illustrates different concepts for providing adaptability in the kitchen. The different height options should correspond with the recommendations given on page 83, based on the specific tasks to be performed.

Adaptable Kitchen Cabinetry Concepts

One concept is the removable cabinet base. In this case, the finished floor should extend under the cabinet. If spanning more than 60 inches [1525 mm], the countertop may need structural reinforcement. Avoid seams by carefully planning the location of the mixing space and sink. A full-height pantry cabinet or nearby closet can be provided to substitute for lost cabinet space after the removal of base cabinets.

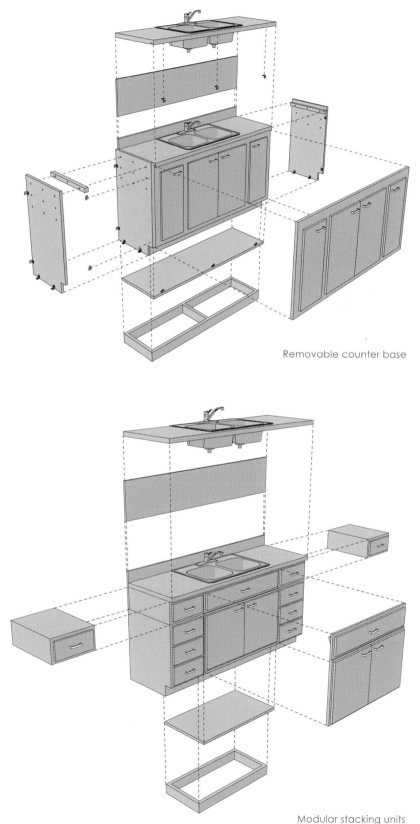

Removable counter base

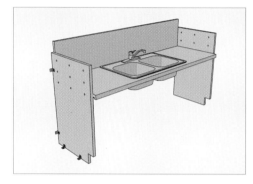

Lower counter after base is removed

Another concept for adaptable cabinetry is the use of modular stacking units. Drawer units can be removable and the counter then lowered to the top of the remaining cabinet section. Like in the previous example, the cabinets and base beneath the sink would be removed to allow knee clearance.

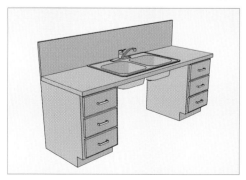

Lower counter supported by modular stacking units with base removed

Modular stacking units

Kitchen Layout `Lifespan`

Galley Kitchen with Knee Space

The minimum clearance for wheelchair access in a kitchen is 40 inches [1025 mm]. A knee clearance under the sink and work area provides a turn-around space and space for seated work. Note that a Fair Housing or Visitable kitchen would not require the turn-around space or knee clearance.

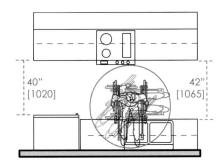

Galley Kitchen with Under-counter Storage

Here, although the circulation clearance is larger, the length of the kitchen is shorter because there is more usable storage under the counters. The work area next to the stove now has a pullout table that provides an additional work space. It also provides a work space with knee clearance for a person using a wheelchair or seated in a chair. Cabinets are provided on both sides of the sink. The wider clearance provides access to the pullout table and increases access to drawers and shelves. Use full extension drawers and pullout shelves for increased usability. This kitchen is large enough for two people to use it comfortably together. This kitchen is also large enough to accommodate a rolling cart that has locking wheels, which provides a movable storage and work surface.

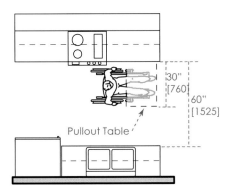

U-shaped Kitchen

A U-shaped kitchen requires a 60 inch [1525 mm] diameter turn-around space for accessibility.

A removable cabinet and base under a counter allows this space to be part of the turn-around space. This also makes the kitchen more usable for two people at once.

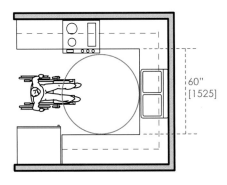

L-shaped Kitchen

This plan is the most convenient because there are no constraints on approach direction nor are there circulation bottlenecks. This usually provides the necessary wheelchair clearances.

An optional island for extra cabinet space or for an accessible mixing surface will provide a boundary between the kitchen and the adjacent rooms, but it limits the approach options. The island can be removable to increase flexibility.

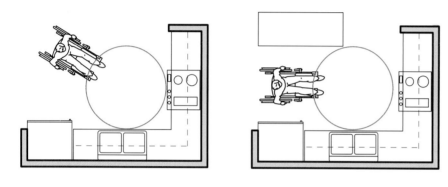

Example of a Lifespan designed kitchen

Image courtesy of John Salmen

SECTION 7

ARCHITECTURAL APPLICATIONS

This section gives examples of different housing types. It covers single- and multifamily housing as well as both Visitable and Lifespan housing. The examples display a range of affordability and house designs suitable for several Transect zones.

Overview

Throughout the book, we emphasized that housing can be accessible without sacrificing urban ideas and aesthetics. This can be accomplished at both a basic Visitable level and a full Lifespan level. It is important to note that only three examples have ramps because the rest are either designed with entries at grade, or the grade is adjusted to meet at least one entry. We included examples with ramps to demonstrate how they can be integrated into designs without negative aesthetic impact. A range of American housing styles that vary in size and cost is illustrated. The first part of this section shows houses that can be built in Transect zones T3 and T4 (suburban to general urban). They are all single-family detached homes. The "Anatomy of a House" example on page 96 provides more detail on common issues that were resolved in every example. The second part of this section shows attached and semi-attached housing designed for Transect zones T3 to T5 (suburban to urban center). It includes a mix of duplexes, townhouses, rowhouses, live-work units, and small apartment buildings. The important features of Visitability and inclusive design that were included in the designs are identified.

Each type of house has its own set of challenges. The major challenge in single-family detached housing is overcoming a misconception about accessible design. Most single-family homes today are built as part of a development plan for an area and are built from basic plans and used multiple times by the same builder. This often means that unless a buyer is disabled and specifically requests modifications to a home, they are not accessible. When a person with a disability purchases a home after construction, they are often forced to make ad-hoc adjustments such as adding ramps. If a customer with a disability requests an "accessible home" from the builder, the builder will often modify a stock plan by simply adding accessibility features like wider doors, larger bathrooms, and a ramp. Few stock plans are designed to be accessible, and builders do not usually re-think the overall design. Thus, misconceptions arise based on past experience. The most common are that either a ramp or a one-story, grade-level design will always be necessary. As we have seen in earlier sections of this book, this is not the case. The second challenge is developing an accessible plan. Often, a house plan that was not accessible can be made accessible simply by rotating a bathroom plan, combining circulation spaces, or moving a wall 6 inches [155 mm]. This is difficult to do once a house is fully designed and certainly once it is already built, but it is easy if planned from the start. The next challenge is to plan ahead to accommodate accessible details at fixtures, appliances, and doorways. The single-family detached housing examples illustrate how these challenges can be overcome.

Attached housing has some additional challenges. Because these houses share walls and are generally narrower than single-family detached houses, there are more limited plan options for accessible entries. Another challenge is the interrelationship of one house to its neighbors. A house on a detached lot can easily have a sloped back or side yard with little or no impact on the neighboring houses. But attached housing requires that the block be planned as a whole. Providing a grade-level entry on one unit usually means it will be easy to do it on all units. This makes a strong case for making all first-floor units accessible. Another challenge is density. The density desired for attached housing usually requires a smaller footprint and at least two stories. Depending on the type of access (Visitable or Lifespan), planning space for a future residential lift or providing an elevator within multistory units or serving several units may need to be considered.

The architectural applications of the recommendations presented in this book demonstrate that the challenges above can be easily overcome without sacrificing marketability, livability, or neighborliness. They will not only provide models that can be readily adopted but also provide a good source of ideas to develop creative solutions to the unique challenges of every design project.

Single-Family Detached Housing Examples

The charts on these two pages index the single-family detached housing examples presented in this section. It is important to keep in mind that there are many possibilities for lot planning, and the sites shown and means of access can often be changed to accommodate diverse sites.

STICK STYLE COTTAGE | Page 94   **Visitable**   **Lifespan**

Building footprint: 1,200 ft² / Habitable space: 1,200 ft²
Bedrooms: 3 / Bathrooms: 2
Lot size: 65 x 90 ft. / 0.13 acre
Transect zones: T3 / T4

AMERICAN CRAFTSMAN BUNGALOW | Page 95   **Visitable**   **Lifespan**

Building footprint: 930 ft² / Habitable space: 1,280 ft²
Bedrooms: 3 / Bathrooms: 2
Lot size: 50 x 95 ft. / 0.11 acre
Transect zones: T3 / T4

MAYBECK INSPIRED BUNGALOW | Page 98   **Visitable**   **Lifespan**

Building footprint: 1,255 ft² / Habitable space: 2,107 ft²
Bedrooms: 3 / Bathrooms: 2
Lot size: 60 x 140 ft. / 0.19 acre
Transect zones: T3 / T4

MAYBECK INSPIRED CARRIAGE HOUSE | Page 99   **Visitable**

Building footprint: 573 ft² / Habitable space: 1,083 ft²
Studio over garage: Bedrooms: 0 / Bathrooms: 1
First-floor apartment: Bedrooms: 1 / Bathrooms: 1
Single two-story apartment: Bedrooms: 2 / Bathrooms 2
Shares lot with Maybeck Inspired Bungalow

TRADITIONAL BUNGALOW | Page 100   **Visitable**   **Lifespan**

Building footprint: 1,343 ft² / Habitable space: 2,157 ft²
Bedrooms: 3 / Bathrooms: 2½
Lot size: 60 x 145 ft. / 0.2 acre
Transect zones: T3 / T4

FRENCH COLONIAL VILLAGE HOME | Page 101

Visitable **Lifespan**

Building footprint: 1,302 ft² / Habitable space: 2,289 ft²
Bedrooms: 3 / Bathrooms: 3
Lot size: 45 x 95 ft. / 0.1 acre
Transect zone: T3 / T4

STICK STYLE FLEXHOUSE™ | Page 102

Visitable **Lifespan**

Building footprint: 1,020 ft² / Habitable space: 2,040 ft²
Single-family house: Bedrooms: 3 / Bathrooms: 3
Two apartments: Bedrooms: 1 / Bathrooms: 1 (per unit)
Lot size: 50 x 100 ft. / 0.11 acre
Transect zones: T3 / T4

NEW ORLEANS SHOTGUN HOME | Page 104

Visitable

Building footprint: 1,833 ft² / Habitable space: 2,766 ft²
Bedrooms: 3 / Bathrooms: 3
Lot size: 40 x 125 ft. / 0.11 acre
Transect zones: T3 / T4

SPANISH COLONIAL REVIVAL MANOR | Page 105

Visitable **Lifespan**

Building footprint: 1,216 ft² / Habitable space: 2,360 ft²
Bedrooms: 3 / Bathrooms: 2¾
Lot size: 50 x 100 ft. / 0.12 acre
Transect zone: T3

FRONTIER MANOR | Page 106

Visitable **Lifespan**

Building footprint: 2,305 ft² / Habitable space: 4,325 ft²
Bedrooms: 5 / Bathrooms: 3½
Lot size: 40 x 110 ft. / 0.1 acre
Transect zone: T3

QUEEN ANNE VICTORIAN MANOR | Page 107

Visitable **Lifespan**

Building footprint: 2,544 ft² / Habitable space: 2,994 ft²
Bedrooms: 6 / Bathrooms: 4
Lot size: 80 x 130 ft. / 0.24 acre
Transect zone: T3

Single Family Detached House
Stick Style Cottage

1,200 ft² building footprint
1,200 ft² habitable space
3 bedroom, 2 bath

Visitable **Lifespan**

Front elevation

Features:

Hidden ramp to front entry **a**
Side driveway or walkway option
Very space-efficient plan
Expanded circulation space in hall
First-floor laundry **b**
Galley kitchen with pass-through
  circulation
1 Visitable bathroom **c**
1 Lifespan bathroom **d**
3 accessible bedrooms

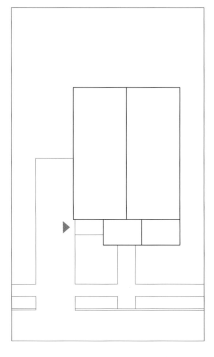

Site plan

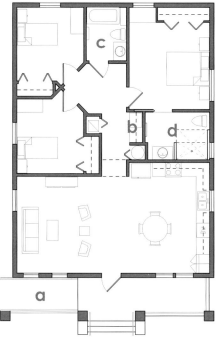

Floor plan

Single-Family Detached House
American Craftsman Bungalow

930 ft² building footprint
1,280 ft² habitable space
3 bedroom, 2 bath

Features:

On-grade front entry with cross-
    sloping lot
Optional on-grade back patio entry
Rear or front driveway option
Generous circulation clearances
Very space-efficient plan
Optional first-floor laundry **a**
L-shaped kitchen
1 Lifespan bathroom **b**
2 accessible bedrooms

Front elevation

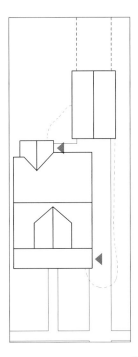

Site plan

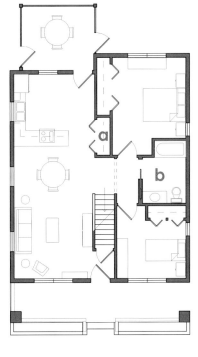

First-floor plan

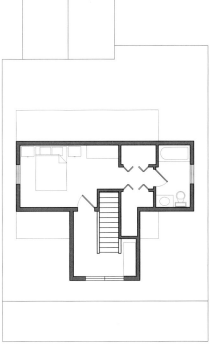

Attic plan

Anatomy of a House

The example on the previous page is the smallest house of our examples. It is a Lifespan home. We developed more extensive drawings of this house to illustrate inclusive design features in depth. The intent is to clearly show how a very small home can be fully accessible. It should be easy to imagine the features that a more elaborate Lifespan home would need. Many of the features shown here will reappear in later examples. This special look at one house will help you better visualize the remaining examples.

Single-Family Detached House
American Craftsman Bungalow

930 ft² building footprint
1,280 ft² habitable space
3 bedroom, 2 bath

Visitable   **Lifespan**

Front elevation

Right side elevation

Rear elevation

Left side elevation

Accessibility does not compromise aesthetics or size

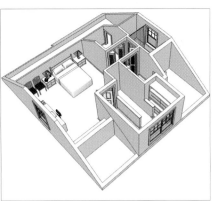

Knee-walls create usable floor space in the attic

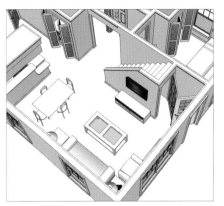

Accessibility does not compromise available space in living areas

Grading provides access to porch and front entry

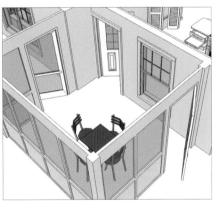

Optional on-grade screened porch

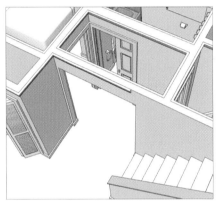

Centralized circulation space and wide passageway

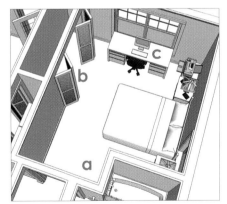

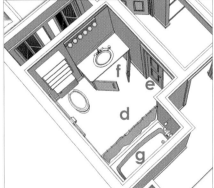

a Spacious bedroom w/ latch-side door clearance

b Bifold doors provide full access to closet

c Ample space for home office furniture and equipment

d Spacious bathroom with 60" turning radius

e Sliding pocket door

f Under-sink knee clearance

g Optional roll-in shower in place of bathtub

h Spacious L-shaped kitchen

i Pullout low work area

j Pullout storage

k Lazy Susan

l Removed base under sink

m Side-by-side refrigerator

Single-Family Detached House
Maybeck Inspired Bungalow

1,255 ft² building footprint
2,107 ft² habitable space
3 bedroom, 2 bath house

 **Visitable** **Lifespan** *

Features:
On-grade front and rear porch entries
Generous circulation clearances
First-floor laundry **a**
Pass-through kitchen
Lifespan bathroom **b**
First-floor bedroom suite
Two-car garage w/ apartment above
Garage can be converted into accessible carriage house (next page)
* Removing outer door and reversing inner door swing will give
  necessary approach clearances for Lifespan housing **c**

Front elevation

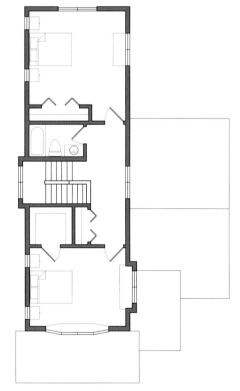

Site plan   First-floor plan   Second-floor plan

Stacked Flat Apartments
Converted Maybeck Inspired Carriage House

573 ft² building footprint
1,083 ft² habitable space
Two 1 bedroom, 1 bath apartments

Visitable

The carriage house has an option for a studio apartment on the second-floor. This gives the house owners the choice to rent it or provide housing in the future for elderly parents, adult children, or even themselves as they age. The plans below demonstrate how the garage level can be transformed into a one-bedroom Visitable apartment. The garage doors would be removed and replaced with windows. Another option is to convert the entire carriage house into one two-story, two-bedroom apartment with a Visitable first-floor and residential elevator.

Front elevation

Converted front elevation

Upper studio apt. plan

Upper studio apt. plan

Second floor of 2BR apt. plan

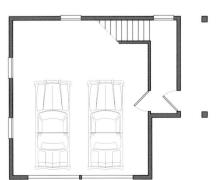

Garage plan

Lower 1BR apt. plan

First floor of 2BR apt. plan

Single-Family Detached House
Traditional Bungalow

1,343 ft^2 building footprint

2,157 ft^2 habitable space

3 bedroom, 2½ bath

Visitable   **Lifespan**

Features:

On-grade rear entry

Optional rear or front driveway

Accessible front porch & rear patio

Extra-wide circulation spaces

Open plan

1 Lifespan bathroom   **a**

1 Visitable half bath or optional first-floor laundry   **b**

Double doors to first-floor bedroom suite

Front elevation

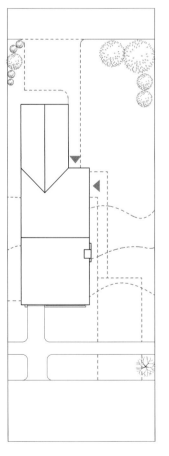

Site plan

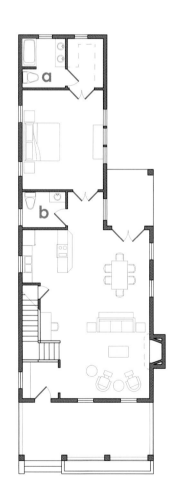

First-floor plan

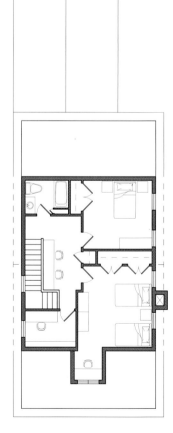

Second-floor plan

Single-Family Detached House
French Colonial Village Home

1,302 ft² building footprint
2,289 ft² habitable space
3 bedroom, 3 bath, 2-car garage

Visitable **Lifespan**

Features:

Ramped rear entry, or sloped garage
  floor for accessible garage entry
Open plan
L-shaped kitchen
1 Lifespan bathroom **a**
Study can convert to small bedroom **b**
Good plan for resort rental house

Front elevation

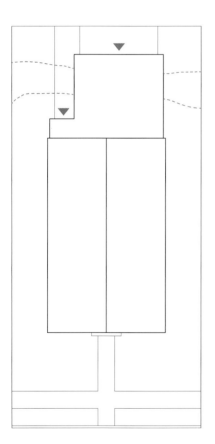

Site plan

First-floor plan

Second-floor plan

Single-Family Detached House (Option)
Stick Style FlexHouse™

1,020 ft² building footprint
2,040 ft² habitable space
3 bedroom, 3 bath house

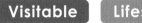
Visitable   **Lifespan**

Features:

On-grade rear entry and patio

Optional sloping grade and walkway
   to front porch (see next page) **a**

Accessible front porch

Open plan

U-shaped kitchen

Lifespan bathroom **b**

Large stacked closets in front entryway could convert to elevator

Ability to convert into stacked flats
   (See option on next page)

Front elevation

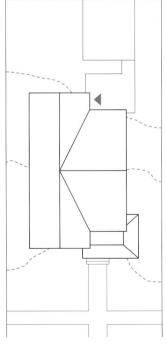

Site plan   First-floor plan   Second-floor plan

Stacked Flat Apartments (Option)
Stick Style FlexHouse™

1,020 ft² building footprint
2,040 ft² habitable space
Two 1 bedroom, 1 bath apartments

The FlexHouse™, a concept developed by the Canadian Mortgage and Housing Corporation, transforms from a single-family home into the stacked flats shown below. A space for a residential elevator is provided in the front of the house. As residents of a household age, they can choose to divide the full house (shown on the previous page) into two apartments with very few changes. The second floor is also accessible so that if a residential elevator is installed, both floors can have Lifespan features. The plans on the previous page show the building as a single-family detached house. The plans below show one way the house can be divided into two apartments. The open plan provides many other possible room arrangements if desired. Because the space for a residential elevator is in the front, if the house is broken into two apartments, the best option for an accessible entry is to have a back driveway with a walkway that slopes up to the front porch. In addition to allowing access to the residential elevator, it provides entry options for the lower unit's occupants. The site plans on each page demonstrate the difference in grading that would make this possible.

Site plan   First-floor plan   Second-floor plan

Single-Family Detached House
New Orleans Shotgun House

1,833 ft² building footprint
2,766 ft² habitable space
3 bedroom, 3 bath

Visitable

Features:
Accessible route to side patio entry
 and/or rear entry
Accessible porches
Spacious living areas
First-floor laundry **a**
Eat-in kitchen
Visitable full bath on first
 floor **b**
Alcoves at front and rear can be
 converted to sleeping spaces **c**
Good plan for narrow lots

Front elevation

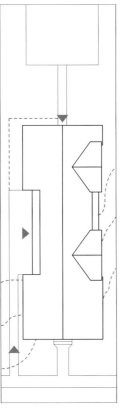

Site plan

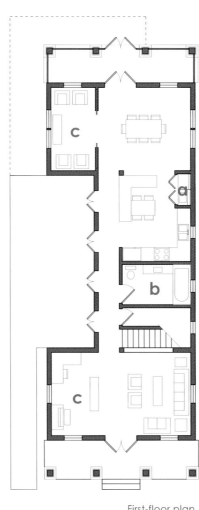

First-floor plan

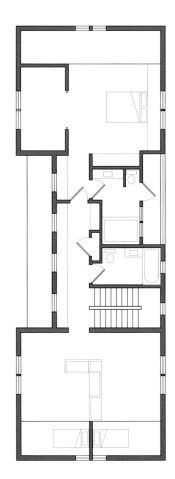

Second-floor plan

Single-Family Detached House
Spanish Colonial Revival Manor

1,216 ft² building footprint
2,360 ft² habitable space
3 bedroom, 2¾ bath

Visitable   **Lifespan**

Features:

On-grade rear entry through garage

Central circulation hall

Generous circulation clearances

First-floor laundry **a**

Lifespan first-floor bath **b**

First-floor den can convert to
bedroom **c**

Front elevation

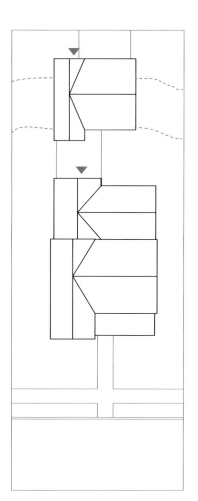

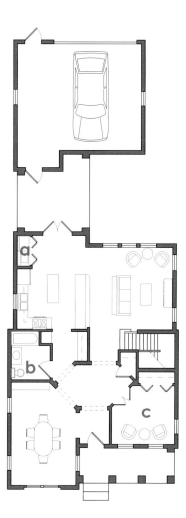

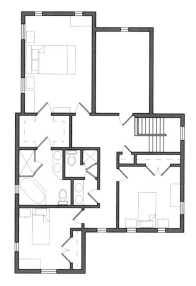

Site plan   First-floor plan   Second-floor plan

Single-Family Detached House
Frontier Manor

2,305 ft² building footprint
4,325 ft² habitable space
5 bedroom, 3½ bath

Visitable **Lifespan**

Features:

On-grade front, rear, and/or
   side entry
Generous circulation clearances
First-floor laundry **a**
Pass-through kitchen
Lifespan bathroom **b**
Living space can be converted
   to bedroom **c**
Elevator can be added if needed

Front elevation

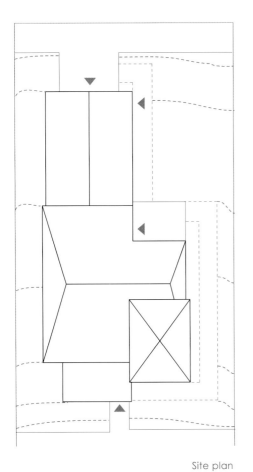

Site plan

First-floor plan

Second-floor plan

Basement-floor plan

Single-Family Detached House
Queen Anne Victorian Manor

2,544 ft² building footprint
2,994 ft² habitable space
6 bedroom, 4 bath

Visitable   **Lifespan**

Features:

Two on-grade rear entry
  options
Generous circulation
  clearances
Open plan
First-floor bedroom suite **a**
First-floor guest bedroom **b**
First-floor laundry **c**
Pass-through kitchen
2 Lifespan bathrooms **d**

Front elevation

This house was significantly altered from an original design of a 4,400-square-foot five-bedroom home with wasted space. The altered design is accessible, has an additional upstairs bedroom, has improved elevations, and a smaller square footage. Not only can careful space planning make a house designed for the lifespan, but it can result in cost savings and generally improved design.

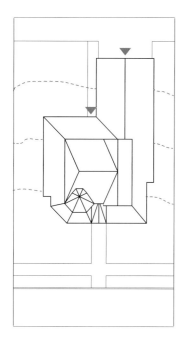

Site plan

First-floor plan

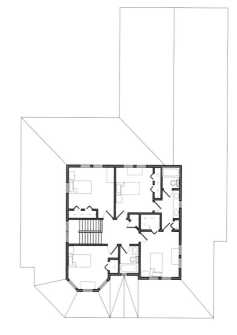

Second-floor plan

Attached Housing Examples

These are charts of the attached housing examples presented in this section. It is important to keep in mind that there are many possibilities for lot planning. The sites shown and approach to accessibility can be adapted to accommodate specific contexts and topography.

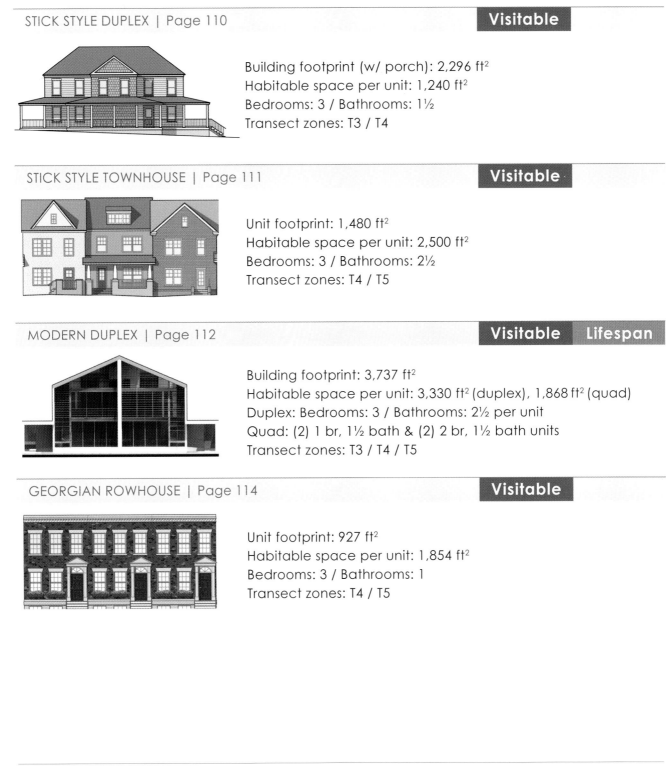

STICK STYLE DUPLEX | Page 110   **Visitable**

Building footprint (w/ porch): 2,296 ft^2
Habitable space per unit: 1,240 ft^2
Bedrooms: 3 / Bathrooms: 1½
Transect zones: T3 / T4

STICK STYLE TOWNHOUSE | Page 111   **Visitable**

Unit footprint: 1,480 ft^2
Habitable space per unit: 2,500 ft^2
Bedrooms: 3 / Bathrooms: 2½
Transect zones: T4 / T5

MODERN DUPLEX | Page 112   **Visitable**   **Lifespan**

Building footprint: 3,737 ft^2
Habitable space per unit: 3,330 ft^2 (duplex), 1,868 ft^2 (quad)
Duplex: Bedrooms: 3 / Bathrooms: 2½ per unit
Quad: (2) 1 br, 1½ bath & (2) 2 br, 1½ bath units
Transect zones: T3 / T4 / T5

GEORGIAN ROWHOUSE | Page 114   **Visitable**

Unit footprint: 927 ft^2
Habitable space per unit: 1,854 ft^2
Bedrooms: 3 / Bathrooms: 1
Transect zones: T4 / T5

LIVE-WORK TOWNHOUSE | Page 115

Visitable

Unit footprint: 1,628 ft^2
Habitable space per unit: 3,600 ft^2
Bedrooms: 3 / Bathrooms: 2½
Transect zones: T4 / T5

NY BROWNSTONE STACKED FLATS | Page 116

Visitable **Lifespan**

Lower unit footprint: 1,100 ft^2
Habitable space per unit: 1,100 ft^2 (lower), 810 ft^2 (upper)
Bedrooms: 2 (upper), 1 (lower) / Bathrooms: 1
Transect zones: T4 / T5

COURTYARD APARTMENTS | Page 117

Visitable **Lifespan**

Building footprint: 5,200 ft^2
Habitable space per flat: 1,420 ft^2
Bedrooms: 2 / Bathrooms: 2 per flat
Transect zone: T5

MIXED-USE APARTMENT BUILDING | Page 118

Visitable

Building footprint: 3,862 ft^2
Habitable space per unit: 1,400–1,800 ft^2
Bedrooms: 2–4 per unit / Bathrooms: 2½ or 3 per unit
Transect zone: T5

Stick Style Duplex

2,296 ft² building footprint (w/ porch)
1,240 ft² habitable interior space per unit
3 bedrooms, 1½ baths per unit

Visitable

Features:

Affordable duplex
Accessible route to porch **a**
Wraparound porch
Separate yards
Spacious open floor plan
U-shaped kitchen
Visitable bathroom **b**

Front elevation

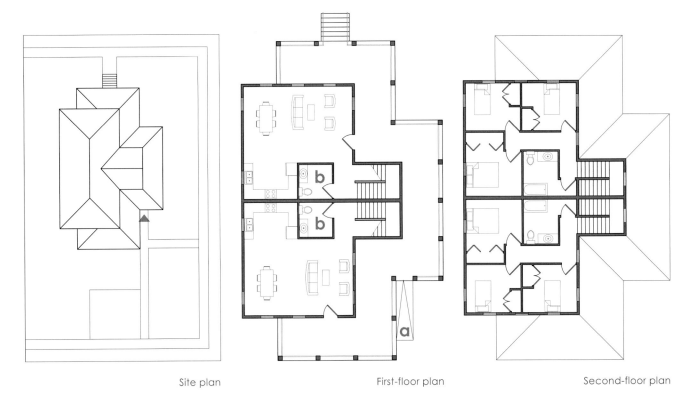

Site plan   First-floor plan   Second-floor plan

Stick Style Townhouse

1,480 ft² building footprint
2,500 ft² habitable space per unit
3 bedroom, 2½ bath

Visitable

Features:
On-grade rear entry through garage
Open plan
First-floor laundry **a**
U-shaped kitchen
Visitable half bath **b**
Space to add first-floor bedroom **c**

Front elevation

Site plan

First-floor plan

Second-floor plan

Site elevation

Modern Duplex

3,737 ft² building footprint
3,330 ft² habitable space per unit*
3 bedroom, 2½ bath per unit

Visitable **Lifespan**

Features:

Semi-attached luxury home for high-density site development

On-grade front and rear entries

Accessible porches and decks

Generous circulation clearances

Optional lifts

Visitable ½ bath **a** Lifespan bath **b**

First-floor bedroom **c**

Two-car garage

Option for one-story units with separate apartments on second-floor

Side porch with reflecting pool and garden wall

Front elevations

First-floor living space

Dining room

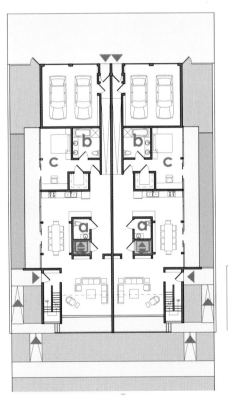

First-floor and site plan

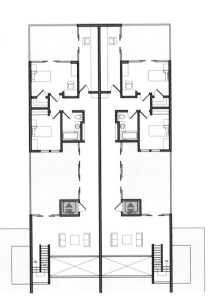

Second-floor plan

Front entrance

Modern Duplex – Apartment Version

3,737 ft² building footprint
1,868 ft² habitable space per unit
(not including attic space)
Two 1 bedroom, 1½ bath units
Two 2 bedroom, 1½ bath units

Visitable   **Lifespan**

This variation includes four separate units. Both floors have the same accessibility features as the single-family version. The first-floor units have use of the garage and side porch. The upstairs units have use of the attic space, a back deck, and a roof terrace.

Roof terrace

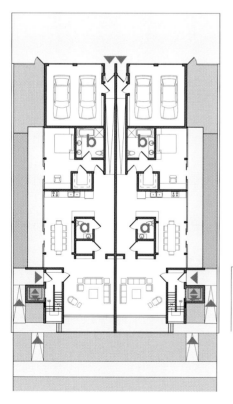

First-floor and site plan

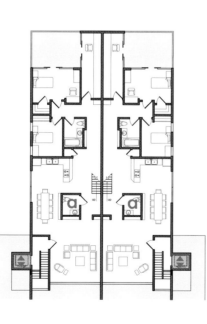

Second-floor plan

Side porch and reflecting pool

Georgian Rowhouse

927 ft² unit footprint
1,854 ft² habitable space per unit
3 bedroom, 1 bath

Visitable

Features:

Traditional narrow urban rowhouse

On-grade rear entry

Generous circulation clearances

U-shaped kitchen

1 Visitable half bath with first-floor laundry **a**

Den could convert to temporary sleeping quarters **b**

Front elevation

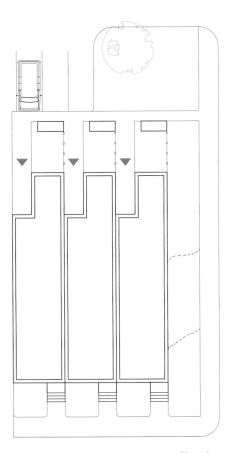

Site plan

First-floor plan

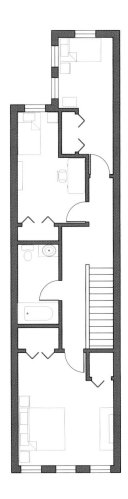

Second-floor plan

Modern Live-Work Townhouse

Front elevation

1,628 ft² unit footprint
3,600 ft² habitable space per unit
3 bedroom, 2½ bath

Visitable

Features:

Double-height work space
Attached 1-car garage with access
  to front work space
On-grade front and rear entries
1 Visitable bathroom **a**

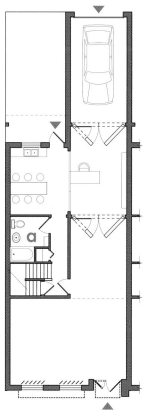

First-floor plan

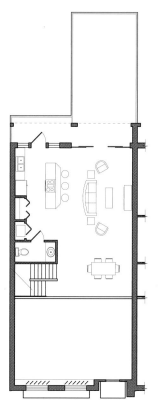

Second-floor plan

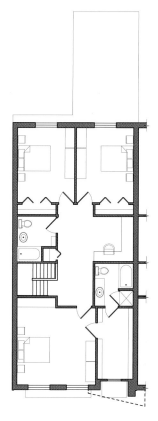

Third-floor plan

New York Brownstone Apartments

1,160 ft² lower unit, 810 ft² upper units
Lower unit: 1 bedroom, 1 bath
Upper units: 2 bedrooms, 1 bath

Visitable   **Lifespan**   (first-floor unit only)

Features:
On-grade front and rear entries
  to first-floor apartment
Spacious living/dining area
Lifespan first-floor bath   **a**

Front elevation

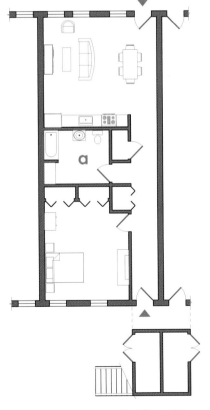

First-floor plan

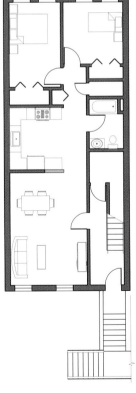

Second-floor plan

Third-floor plan

Courtyard Apartments

5,200 ft² building footprint
1,380 ft² habitable space per unit
Two 2 bedroom, 2 bath units
Four 2-story 3 bedroom, 3 bath units

Visitable   **Lifespan**

Features:

On-grade courtyard access
Shared courtyard **a**
Shared multi-car garage **b**
2 first-floor units
Optional laundry **c**
Pass-through kitchen
1 Lifespan bathroom **d**
1 Visitable bathroom **e**
Master bedroom suite **f**

*Note: All apartment complexes
with more than four units must
comply with Fair Housing Laws

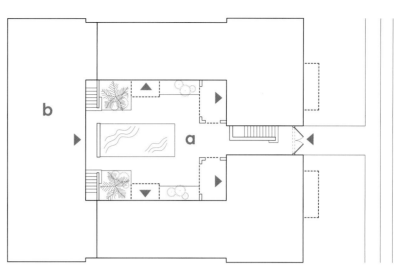

Site plan

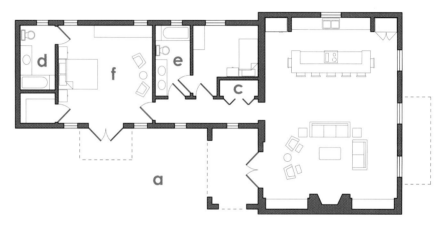

Floor plan (apartments)

Section

Mixed-Use / Live-Work

3,862 ft² building footprint

Unit 1 & 2: 1,800 ft² per unit
  Retail space
  3 bedrooms, 2½ baths
  2 stories
  optional elevator

Unit 3 & 4: 1,400 ft² per unit
  2 bedrooms, 2½ baths
  2 stories
  optional elevator

Unit 5 & 6: 1,700 ft² per unit
  4 bedrooms, 3 baths
  elevator access

Side elevation

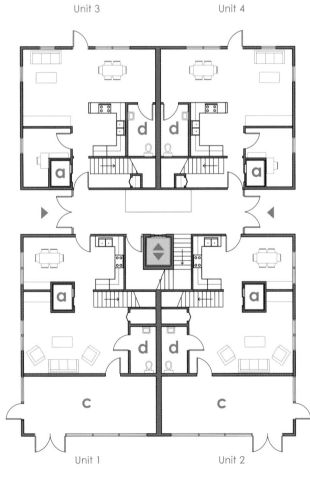

First-floor plan

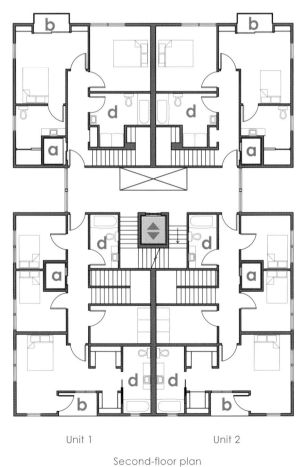

Second-floor plan

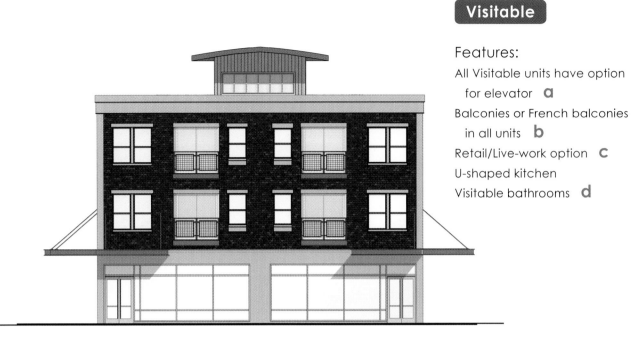

Front elevation

Visitable

Features:

All Visitable units have option
for elevator **a**

Balconies or French balconies
in all units **b**

Retail/Live-work option **c**

U-shaped kitchen

Visitable bathrooms **d**

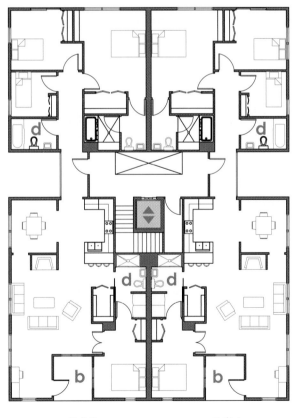

Unit 5   Unit 6

Third-floor plan

*Note: All apartment complexes
with more than four units must
comply with Fair Housing Laws

SECTION 8

APPENDICES

This section of the book contains the appendices referenced in the book as well as additional resources to the topics covered. The end of this section contains the index and acknowledgments.

Appendix A: ICC Type C Units

This is a summary of the first ICC/ANSI A117.1 standard for Visitable dwelling units. Section numbers listed correspond to sections in the standard. The language of the standard is simplified here to be concise and easy-to-understand. Key cross references to other sections of the standard are included. See the full standard for the complete text.

Type C Units (Section 1006)

The purpose of Type C requirements is to provide a model standard that can be adopted for application to single-family homes that are not covered by the Fair Housing Act. Local authorities are encouraged to consider exemptions where conditions such as extreme topographical conditions warrant them. The application of Type C (Visitability) criteria is based on widespread, i.e. universal, application to primarily owner-occupied dwellings. There is currently no scoping for the Type C Unit in the International Building Code (IBC). Type C criteria are intended for use by states or municipalities that are interested in adopting Visitability legislation.

Unit Entrance (1006.2)

At least one unit entrance shall be on a circulation path complying with Section 1006.5 (Circulation Path) from a public street or sidewalk, a dwelling-unit driveway, or a garage.

Connected & Interior Spaces (1006.3 & 1006.4)

A circulation path complying with Section 1006.5 (Circulation Path) shall connect the unit entrance located on the circulation path to:

a. An entrance-level toilet room or bathroom complying with Section 1006.6 (Toilet Room or Bathroom).

b. One additional habitable space with an area 70 square feet [6.5 m²] minimum.

c. When provided on the entrance level, a food preparation area complying with Section 1006.7 (Food Preparation Areas).

Exception: A toilet room or bathroom shall not be required in units with less than 120 square feet [11 m²] of habitable space on the entrance level.

Circulation Path (1006.5)

Components (1006.5.1): The circulation path shall include one or more of the following elements: walking surfaces with a slope not steeper than 1:20, doors and doorways, ramps, compliant elevators (Section 407-409), and compliant platform lifts (Section 410).

Walking Surfaces (1006.5.2) and **Thresholds (1006.5.3.2):** Thresholds and slopes not steeper than 1:20 shall comply with Section 303 (Changes in Level). Section 303.2 permits abrupt changes in level up to ¼ inch [6.4 mm]. Section 303.3 states, "Changes in level greater than ¼ inch [6.4 mm] in height and less than ½ inch [13 mm] maximum in height shall be beveled with a slope no greater than 1:2. Changes in level greater than ½ inch [13 mm] in height shall be ramped and comply with Section 405 (Ramps) or 406 (Curb Ramps)."

> **Exception:** Thresholds at exterior sliding doors shall be permitted to be ¾ inch [19 mm] maximum in height, provided they are beveled with a slope not steeper than 1:2.

Clear Width (1006.5.2.1): The clear width of the circulation path shall comply with Section 403.5 (Clear Width) which states, hallways and corridors must have at least 36 inches [915 mm] clear width.

> **Exception:** Pinch points are allowed to be 32 inches [815 mm] for a distance of 24 inch [610 mm] maximum (see figure).

Doors and Doorways (1006.5.3.1): Swinging doors shall have a clear opening of 31 ¾ inches [810 mm] minimum measured from the jamb to the inside face of the door and stop with the door open at 90 degrees. Sliding and folding doors shall be measured from the jamb to the inside edge of the door in the open position. Automated doors may be used if they meet all applicable code requirements, including the requirements in ICC/ANSI A117.1.

> **Exception:** Doorways to closets with 15 square feet [1.4 m²] space maximum.

Ramps (1006.5.4): Ramps shall comply with Section 405 (Ramps).

> **Exception:** Handrails, intermediate landings, and edge protection are not required where the sides of ramp runs have a vertical drop-off of ½ inch [13 mm] maximum within 10 inches [255 mm] horizontally of a ramp run.

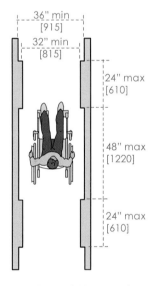

Clear width exception:
Pinch points (short, narrower areas)

Toilet Room or Bathroom (1006.6)

Toilet rooms or bathrooms covered by Section 1006.4 (Interior Spaces) shall include the following features:

a. A lavatory and a toilet.

b. Reinforcement and space clearances for the future installation of grab bars at toilets.

Note: If more than one bathroom is provided on the entry floor, reinforcement is required in at least one full bathroom on that floor.

c. The wall reinforced for the future installation of grab bars shall be 18 inches [455 mm] from the centerline of the toilet.

d. Lavatories must be at least 15 inches [380 mm] from the centerline of the toilet.

e. Space clearances at the toilet must meet or exceed the minimum requirements for at least one of the following sections:

"Parallel Approach" (1004.11.3.1.2.1):

i. Measured from the wall behind the toilet, there shall be a minimum clear space of 56 inches [1420 mm].

ii. Measured from the wall designated for the future installation of grab bars, there shall be a minimum clear space of 48 inches [1220 mm].

iii. Vanities or lavatories beside the toilet may overlap required space clearances.

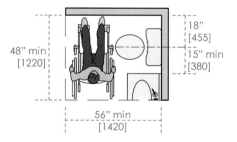

Parallel approach

"Forward Approach" (1004.11.3.1.2.2):

i. Measured from the wall behind the toilet, there shall be a minimum clear space of 66 inches [1680 mm].

ii. Measured from the wall designated for the future installation of grab bars, there shall be a minimum clear space of 48 inches [1220 mm].

iii. Vanities or lavatories beside the toilet may overlap required space clearances.

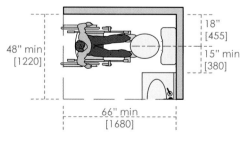

Forward approach

"Parallel or Forward Approach" (1004.11.3.1.2.3):

> **i.** Measured from the wall behind the toilet, there shall be a minimum clear space of 56 inches [1420 mm].

> **ii.** Measured from the centerline of the toilet, there shall be a minimum clear space of 42 inches [1065 mm].

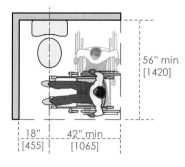

Parallel or forward approach

Food Preparation Areas (1006.7)

> **a.** When provided on the entrance level, the food preparation area shall include a sink, a cooking appliance, and a refrigerator.

> **b.** Clearances between all opposing base cabinets, countertops, appliances, or walls within the food preparation area shall be 40 inches [1015 mm] minimum.

> **Exception:** Spaces that do not have a cooktop or conventional range shall be permitted to have a minimum clearance of 36 inches [915 mm] wide.

Lighting Controls & Receptacle Outlets (1006.8)

The centerline of receptacle outlets and operable parts of lighting controls shall be located a minimum of 15 inches [380 mm] and a maximum of 48 inches [1220 mm] above the finished floor.

> **Exception:** The following shall not be required to comply with Section 1006.8:

> **1.** Receptacle outlets serving a dedicated use (e.g. outlets intended for refrigerators or laundry equipment)

> **2.** Controls mounted on ceiling fans and ceiling lights

> **3.** Floor receptacle outlets

> **4.** Lighting controls and receptacle outlets over countertops

Appendix B: Wall Section Details

In typical residential construction in the United States, foundation walls extend 6 inches above grade and the floor system is framed either into or on top of it. In order to create a no-step entry, conventional detailing can be replaced with a "reverse brick ledge." In this design, the foundation is notched around the framing, such that the finish floor is nearly flush with the top of the foundation.

If the foundation is designed this way, exterior wall finish materials are brought closer to grade. However, unprotected exterior finish materials must be at least 6 inches above grade. Thus, protecting walls adjacent to the entry from water penetration must be considered. The details illustrate different approaches to protection.

A method commonly used for masonry construction in the United Kingdom is a damp proof course. A thin plastic sheet is inserted between brick courses 6 inches above grade. This sheet prevents water from rising up the wall. The damp proof course material extends down the wall under a slab or grade or down the face of basement walls to prevent moisture from infiltrating the floor.

Another technique is to install a gravel-filled trench around the perimeter of the building. This is illustrated in the details with siding as a finish material, but it could be used with any material. Any rainwater or melting snow that reaches the foundation runs quickly down the perimeter storm drainage system. This ensures that no water pools around the building.

Each set of section details is referred to using the locations in the diagram below.

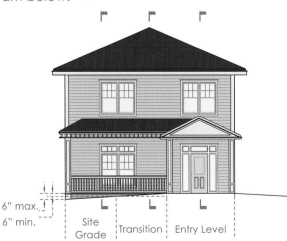

6" max.
6" min.
Site Grade   Transition   Entry Level

▶ Note: Vapor barrier placement varies by region, so its location is not always shown in these details. Check local building codes and practices.

Slab on Grade with Wooden Studs & Brick Veneer

Wall Section at Site Grade:

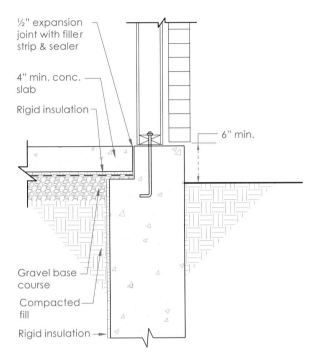

½" expansion joint with filler strip & sealer

4" min. conc. slab

Rigid insulation

6" min.

Gravel base course

Compacted fill

Rigid insulation

Wall Section at Transition:

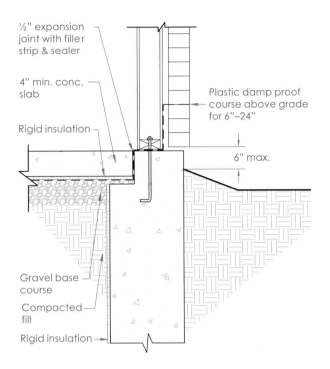

½" expansion joint with filler strip & sealer

4" min. conc. slab

Rigid insulation

Plastic damp proof course above grade for 6"–24"

6" max.

Gravel base course

Compacted fill

Rigid insulation

Wall Section at Entry:

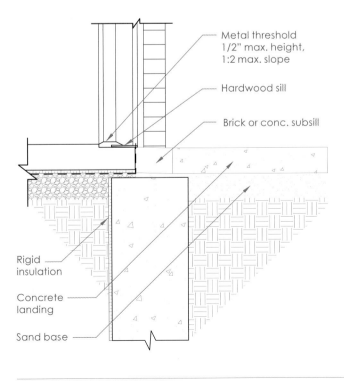

Metal threshold 1/2" max. height, 1:2 max. slope

Hardwood sill

Brick or conc. subsill

Rigid insulation

Concrete landing

Sand base

Notes:

▶ Stud wall construction

▶ Brick veneer on exterior wall

▶ Roof at entry is desirable to reduce water and snow buildup at entry landing

▶ Subsill provides flexibility for adjustment if foundation or landing shifts

▶ Damproofing used for added protection

Basement or Crawl Space with Wooden Studs & Siding

Wall Section at Site Grade:

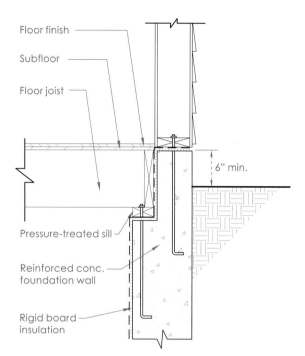

Floor finish

Subfloor

Floor joist

6" min.

Pressure-treated sill

Reinforced conc. foundation wall

Rigid board insulation

Wall Section at Transition:

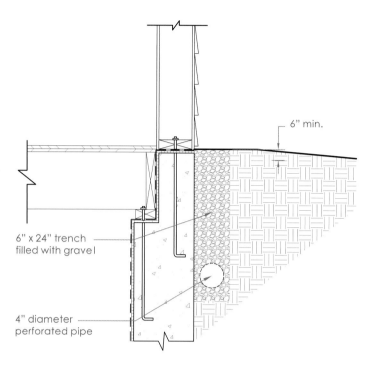

6" min.

6" x 24" trench filled with gravel

4" diameter perforated pipe

Wall Section at Entry:

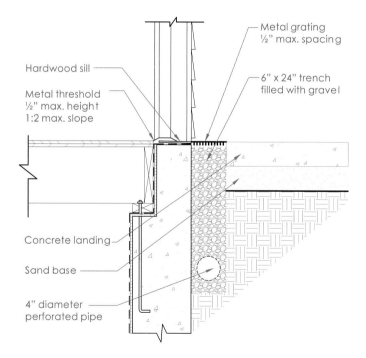

Hardwood sill

Metal threshold ½" max. height 1:2 max. slope

Metal grating ½" max. spacing

6" x 24" trench filled with gravel

Concrete landing

Sand base

4" diameter perforated pipe

Notes:

▶ Stud wall construction

▶ Wooden siding on exterior wall

▶ Reverse brick ledge lowers floor framing

▶ Gravel-filled trench and perimeter drain create positive drainage

▶ Metal grate bridges gravel at entry

▶ Solid paver could be substituted for grate

Basement or Crawl Space with Wooden Studs & Brick Veneer

Wall Section at Site Grade:

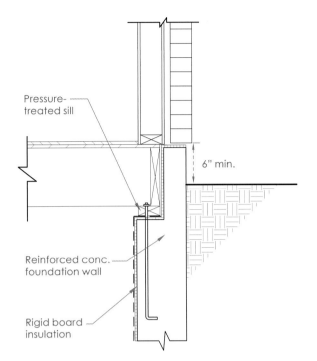

Pressure-treated sill

6" min.

Reinforced conc. foundation wall

Rigid board insulation

Wall Section at Transition:

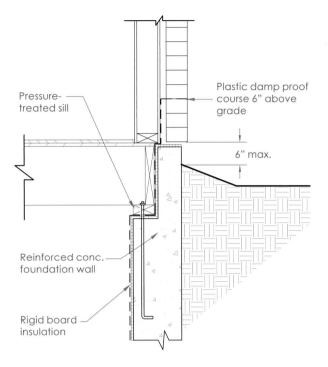

Pressure-treated sill

Plastic damp proof course 6" above grade

6" max.

Reinforced conc. foundation wall

Rigid board insulation

Wall Section at Entry:

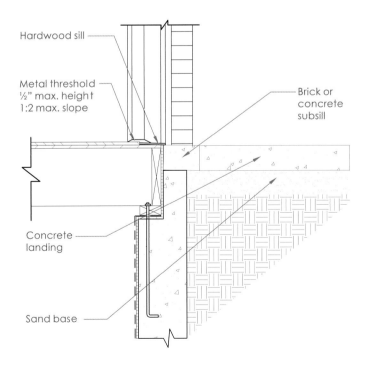

Hardwood sill

Metal threshold
½" max. height
1:2 max. slope

Brick or concrete subsill

Concrete landing

Sand base

Notes:

▶ Stud wall construction

▶ Brick veneer on exterior wall

▶ Reverse brick ledge lowers floor framing

▶ Gravel-filled trench and perimeter drain create positive drainage

▶ Metal grate bridges gravel at entry

▶ Solid paver could be substituted for grate

On-Grade Entry Details

This set of details compares typical construction details (top) with accessible details.

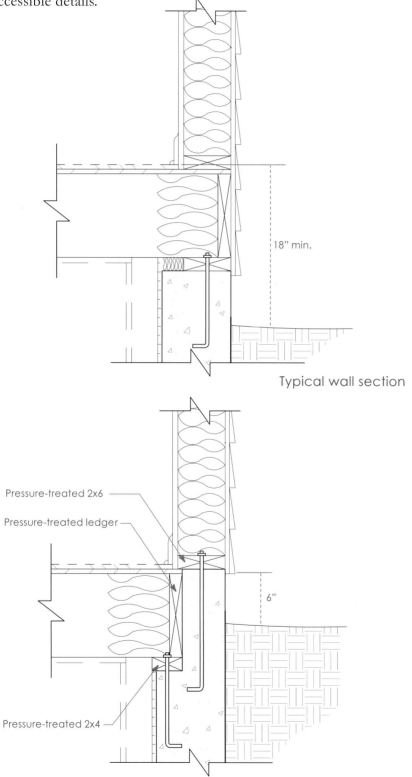

18" min.

Typical wall section

Pressure-treated 2x6

Pressure-treated ledger

6"

Pressure-treated 2x4

Section at site grade with reverse brick ledge foundation

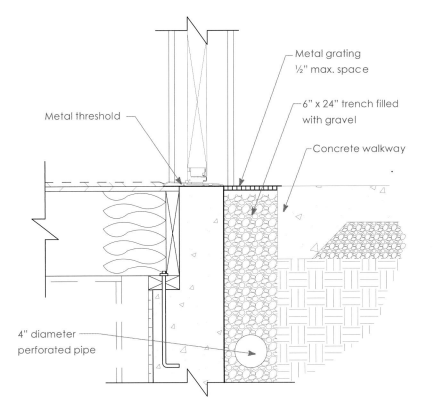

Metal grating
½" max. space

6" x 24" trench filled
with gravel

Concrete walkway

Metal threshold

4" diameter
perforated pipe

Section at landing entry with reverse brick ledge foundation

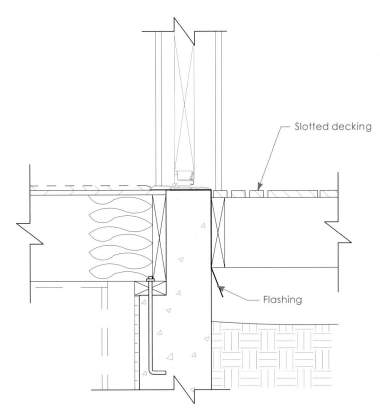

Slotted decking

Flashing

Section at porch entry with reverse brick ledge foundation

Deck Entry Proposals

A reverse brick ledge detail is not needed if access will be provided through a deck or porch raised off grade. This set of details compares a typical porch or deck entry with accessible versions. The top example shows a sliding glass door. The bottom shows a swinging door with a low threshold.

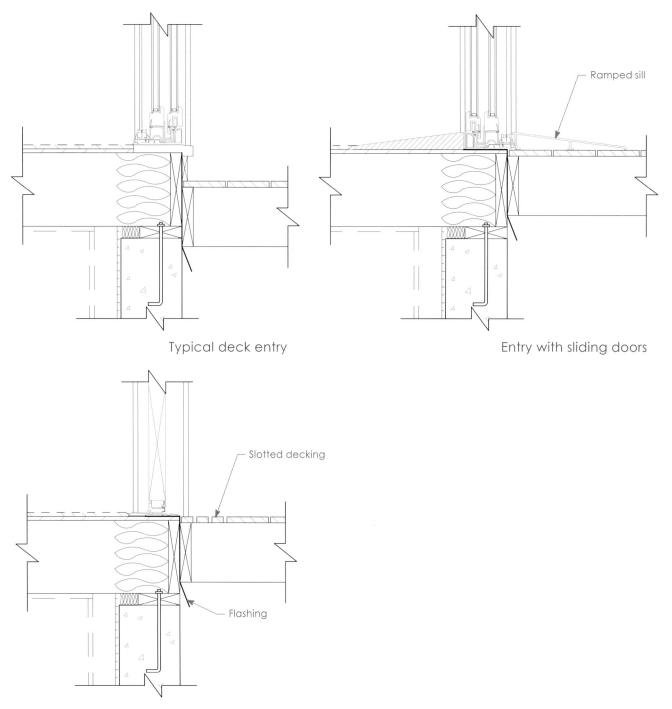

Ramped sill

Typical deck entry

Entry with sliding doors

Slotted decking

Flashing

Entry with patio door

Alternative to Reverse Brick Ledge

This page shows an alternative to the proposed "reverse brick ledge" foundation. A vapor barrier between the stone and treated lumber keeps moisture from damaging the wood structures. This detail is not recommended in areas with termites. A pressure-treated trim board is used to protect the structural lumber.

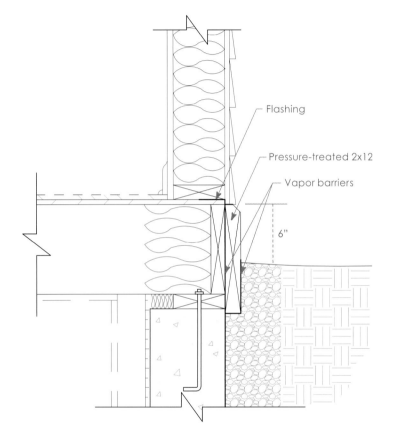

Flashing

Pressure-treated 2x12

Vapor barriers

6"

Pressure-treated trim board protecting structure

References

Bostrom, J., Corning, B., Mace, R., Long, M. (1987). *Adaptable Housing: Marketable Accessible Housing for Everyone.* Washington, DC: U.S. Department of Housing and Urban Development, Office of Policy Development and Research.

Concrete Change. (2004). *Builder Exec Affirms Low Cost of Visitability!!* Retrieved on November 30, 2007, from http://www.con cretechange.org/buildersaffirm.htm.

Danford, G. Scott and Steinfeld, E. (1999). *Measuring the Influences of Physical Environments on the Behaviors of People with Impairments.* Steinfeld, E., and Danford, G. S. (eds.). Measuring Enabling Environments, New York: Kluwer Academic/Plenum. 111–136.

Ellis, Cliff. (2002). "The New Urbanism: Critiques and Rebuttals." *Journal of Urban Design,* Vol. 7, No. 3. 261–291.

Faar, D. (2007). *Sustainable Urbanism: Urban Design with Nature.* New York: John Wiley & Sons, Inc.

Fischel, W. A. (2004). "An Economic History of Zoning and a Cure For Its Exclusionary Effects." *Urban Studies,* 41. 317–340.

Frey, W. (2001). *City Families and Suburban Singles: An Emerging Household Story from Census 2000.* Brookings Institution (21 July 2005). http://www.brookings.edu/ed/urban/census/freyfamiliesexec sum.htm.

IDEA Center. (2006). Telephone Survey. Buffalo: University at Buffalo, School of Architecture and Planning.

Maisel, J., Smith, E., and Steinfeld, E. (2008). *In Brief: Increasing Home Access: Designing for Visitability.* AARP Public Policy Paper. http://www.aarp.org/research/housing-mobility/accessibility/inb163_access.html.

Michelson, W. (1977). *Environmental Choice, Human Behavior, and Residential Satisfaction.* New York: Oxford University Press.

Newman, O. (1972). *Defensible Space.* New York: Macmillan.

Norman, D. (2004). *Emotional Design: Why We Love (or Hate) Everyday Things.* New York: Basic Books.

Randolph, J. (2003). *Environmental Land Use Planning and Management.* Washington, DC: Island Press.

Smith, S. K., Rayer, S., and Smith, E. A. (2008). "Aging and Disability: Implications for the Housing Industry and Public Policy in the United States." *Journal of the American Planning Association,* Summer 2008, Vol. 74, No. 3.

Steinfeld, E., Schroeder, S., and Bishop, M. (1979). *Adaptable Dwellings.* Prepared for the U.S. Department of Housing and Urban Development, Office of Policy Development and Research.

Stephen Winter & Associates, Inc. (2001). *A Basic Guide to Fair Housing Accessibility: Everything Architects and Builders Need to Know About the Fair Housing Act Accessibility Guidelines.* New York: John Wiley & Sons, Inc.

Stephen Winter & Associates, Inc. (1993). *Cost of Accessible Housing: An Analysis of the Estimated Cost of Compliance with the Fair Housing Accessibility Guidelines and ANSI A 117.1.* Prepared for the U. S. Department of Housing and Urban Development. Washington, DC: U.S. Department of Housing and Urban Development, Office of Policy Development and Research.

U.S. Census Bureau. (2004). *Population projections: U.S. Interim Projections by Age, Sex, Race, and Hispanic Origin: 2000–2050.* Retrieved on June 26, 2008, from http://www.census.gov/ipc/www/usin terimproj/.

U.S. Census Bureau. (2001). *American Housing Survey.* Retrieved on October 2, 2007, from http://www.census.gov/hhes/www/housing/ahs/ahs01_2000wts/ahs01_2000wts.html.

Williams, T., and Altaffer, W. (2000). *Cost Analysis Review for Proposed Visitability Ordinance.* Tucson, AZ: Commission on Disability Issues.

World Health Organization. (2006). *Disability and Rehabilitation.* WHO Action Plan 2006–2011.

Wylde, M. (2002). *Boomers on the Horizon: Housing Preferences of the 55+ Market.* Washington, DC: National Association of Home Builders.

Acknowledgments

Text by Edward Steinfeld and Jonathan White, with contributions from: Danise Levine, Jordana Maisel, Heamchand Subryan, John Sepples, Danielle McCrossen, Stephanie Koch, and David Schoell

Special thanks to members of our advisory panel for their input and suggestions: Murphy Antoine, Katherine Austin, Victor Deupi, Bruce Donnelly, Terri O'Hare, Eric Osth, Eleanor Smith, Korydon SMith, and Louis Tenenbaum.

Photo credits: Google (pages 18 and 19) and John Salmen (page 87).
Design credit: Mississippi Renewal Housing Designs; Erika Albright and Matthew Lister (page 31).

Credits for Home Designs in Section 7 (Architectural Applications)

p. 94: Stick Style Cottage
Original design copyright © New Millennial, LC
Revisions by Danielle McCrossen and Jonathan White

pp. 95–97: American Craftsman Bungalow
Original design by Jonathan White

pp. 98–99: Maybeck Inspired Bungalow and Carriage House
Original design by Katherine Austin, AIA
Revisions by Linfan Liu,* Danielle McCrossen, and Jonathan White

p. 100: Traditional Bungalow
Original design by Lew Oliver
Revisions by Alex Kwa* and Jonathan White

p. 101: French Colonial Village Home
Original design by David Weekley Homes
Revisions by Yuxiang Xiao* and Jonathan White

p. 102: Stick Style FlexHouse™ and Apartments
Original design by Jonathan White

p. 104: New Orleans Shotgun Home
Original design by Edward Steinfeld

p. 105: Spanish Colonial Revival Manor
Original design by Cambridge Homes
Revisions by Erin Rossier* and Jonathan White

p. 106: Frontier Manor
Original design by Harvard Communities
Revisions and illustrations by Stephanie Koch

p. 107: Queen Anne Victorian Manor
Significant alterations by Jonathan White*

p. 110: Stick Style Duplex
Original design by Mason Andrews
Revisions by Elizabeth Gerber* and Danielle McCrossen

p. 111: Stick Style Townhouse
Original design by Katherine Austin, AIA
Revisions by John Sepples and Danielle McCrossen

p. 112: Modern Duplex
Original design and illustrations by Yuxiang Xiao*
Revisions by Jonathan White

p. 114: Georgian Rowhouse
Original design by John Sepples
Revisions by Jonathan White

p. 115 Live-Work Townhouse
Original design by John Sepples and Jonathan White

p. 116: New York Brownstone Apartments
Original design by John Sepples
Revisions by Jonathan White

p. 117: Courtyard Apartments
Original design by Duany Plater-Zyberk & Company
Revisions by Jonathan White

pp. 118–19: Mixed-Use Apartment Building
Original design and illustrations by Stephanie Koch

Unless otherwise noted, all Section 7 illustrations by Jonathan White and Danielle McCrossen

* Substantial revisions or original design by named student prior to IDEA staff revisions

Index